Juror Number Three

Sixth Amendment to the Constitution
of the United States of America

In all criminal prosecutions, the accused shall enjoy the right to a speedy and public trial, by an impartial jury of the state and district wherein the crime shall have been committed, which district shall have been previously ascertained by law, and to be informed of the nature and cause of the accusation; to be confronted with the witnesses against him; to have compulsory process for obtaining witnesses in his favor, and to have the assistance of counsel for his defense.

Juror Number Three

Linda Johnson

Event Horizon Press • Albuquerque, New Mexico USA

Juror Number Three

Book Design Copyright © 2015 Event Horizon Press
www.eventhorizonpress.com

Designed by and Edited by Joseph Robert Cowles
Produced by Barbora Holan Cowles

Cover Images © Bigstock

Some names, characterizations and circumstances presented herein
(excluding court testimony and evidence) have been altered
to conceal the identities of the persons involved.

ISBN-13: 978-1517570934
ISBN-10:151757093X

This book is dedicated to my family and friends
who were supportive of my efforts to write this book,
and to the importance of the role of the juror
in the guiding principles of justice in our country.

Foreword

Serving on the jury of a murder trial, knowing my actions might result in the death penalty, was an incredibly intense experience. When I first started to write my notes, I did it to debrief myself, express some of my thoughts, and just decompress so that I could gain closure and get on with my life. In the first few days following the end of the trial, I discovered that some of my friends and coworkers were very interested in the details of this case, and were more than politely encouraging when I began to share some of the information from the trial which was not necessarily reported in the news.

Writing my notes and impressions turned out to be a much bigger project than I had imagined; only a few weeks after the trial ended, my recollection was already starting to fade. I've tried to give as accurate an account as I can of my impressions of the trial. I've also tried to give a fair representation of my fellow jurors and I ask their indulgence if I've not portrayed their views or actions as they would have. Everyone on this jury was sincere and dedicated and gave this case their absolute best effort. Out of respect for their privacy, I've changed the names of the jurors.

This book is structured to enable the reader of this account to gain insight into what the jury process is like for an individual juror. As you read the jury instructions, testimony, evidence and exhibits shared in these pages, you will be able to determine what your own decision might have been as a juror on this case.

My goal in writing this book has been to entertain and to educate. It is my hope that the reader will enjoy learning about the challenges of serving on a jury and will develop appreciation and compassion for those called upon to do so. In today's society, there is an ever-increasing chance that you the reader may be the one called upon.

— Linda Johnson

Part 1

The Summons

I came home from work one day, and there it was. A summons for jury duty for Arizona Superior Court in Maricopa County. I had been asked to take on additional responsibilities at work and really didn't need the interruption. I set the summons aside so it wouldn't get lost in the stack of mail. A couple of days later I decided I'd better not wait too long to take a look at it because I knew there must be a deadline for my response. The date to appear was August 15th. There were satellite court locations, but my summons was for the downtown Phoenix location, only a short distance from my work. I thought about asking for a postponement because I remembered I had to be in Tucson on August 17th. Then, after closer inspection, I decided I would have a better chance of avoiding jury duty if I did appear on the 15th. The summons explained the court's "one day/one trial" policy in which you only have to show up for the one day of jury selection. If you are chosen to serve on a jury, most trials only last a day or two. Equally important, if your schedule limits your availability, you can be excused.

A decade earlier I had served on a jury in federal court for a criminal trial that lasted over five weeks. It had been very difficult to work intermittently at my job for such an extended period; no way did I want to go through that experience again. But if I just had to serve for a day or two, I would allow my sense of civic duty to prevail. I thought that if the trial were to be longer than a couple of days, I could legitimately be excused from jury duty because of my meeting in Tucson.

I also thought I had an "ace in the hole" because of my prior jury duty service. Jury selection includes a voir dire (literally, "to speak the truth") process in which jurors are asked questions about their background, whether they know anyone involved in the case, etc. Jurors are eliminated if they are challenged for cause; for example, if they are related to someone involved in the case. Both the prosecution and defense attorneys also have a limited number of peremptory challenges. I'd received a jury summons not long after the federal court case, and one of the voir dire questions asked whether anyone had served on a jury previously. Those who raised their hand were asked what type of case (criminal or civil), whether the jury reached a verdict, and what the verdict was. I was in the jury box and could only be excused if eliminated by a challenge. After I responded that I'd been on a jury that reached a verdict of guilty in a criminal case, I was excused. I confidently filled out my summons for August 15th and mailed it back to Superior Court. There should be no problem.

Juror Selection

The day of my summons was a Monday. I showed up at about my appointed time of 9:30 a.m., stood in a fairly long but fast-moving line to go through security, and reported to the jury assembly room. The large room was already filled with people and barely a spare seat was to be found. I went up to the reception desk, signed in, took an information sheet, and looked for a place to sit down. I'd brought my laptop with me so I could get some work done in case it turned out to be a long day of waiting. There were TV monitors stationed throughout the room that were set to various morning shows.

By about ten o'clock, some action finally started to take place. The court staff played an orientation video for the prospective jurors. It explained there were both civil and criminal trials, and some of the differences between them. It put a lot of emphasis on the importance of jury duty for our judicial system's right to a trial by a jury of your peers. As much as I didn't want to be there, it's hard to overlook the importance of trial by jury—especially when you look around and see what is happening in other parts of the world.

Shortly after the orientation video, the monitors were put on pause and court staff announced that they would be calling off names to form a jury panel. Everyone sat quietly and listened, waiting to hear if their name would be called. As the names were called off, the prospective jurors were asked to remember the number assigned to them. A total of thirty-six names were called. Mine was not one of them. So far so good.

The morning shows were now over, so the court staff inserted a video and all of the TV monitors started showing the movie, "Miss Congeniality." Entertainment was fine with me and I settled in, wondering how long my day in the jury assembly room would be. I noticed a whiteboard at the back of the room, indicating that there would be ten cases going to trial that day. I looked around and tried to determine the number of people. The room looked like it might hold three hundred. Several jury panels would be formed and assigned to various courts, and at thirty-six per panel, the odds of not being selected for a panel didn't seem very good.

Soon the court staff started the process again, calling out thirty-six more names, again asking each person to remember the assigned juror number. Almost immediately a third panel was selected, but this time fifty names were called off. Once more, my name was not among those called. I was particularly happy not to be on the list of fifty as I speculated that the larger size of the panel probably meant the trial would require more time. I settled back into my routine of watching the movie. Throughout the morning, additional jury panels were called and sent off to various locations within the court complex. Still, my name wasn't called. Once again, so far so good.

I had probably been waiting around in the jury assembly room for about an hour and a half when it was time for yet another panel to be called. As the count reached the high twenties, I began to feel hopeful that I would once again dodge the jury-panel bullet. But this time, my name was the twenty-ninth to be called. Much to my dismay, the names continued to be called until there were fifty in my group. I picked up my things, walked over to the staging area and waited to be herded to another location in the central court building.

Our bailiff, Larry Martinez, introduced himself, asked everyone to stay together, and told us we were going to the eleventh floor. We started down the corridor toward the central bank of elevators. Upon our arrival on the eleventh floor, we were directed around the corner to the front entrance of the courtroom and asked to wait. Fifty people looked for a vacant bench on which to sit, or a place along the corridor to stand and wait. Larry also recruited one of the prospective jurors and asked her to collect everyone's jury assignment sheet and put them in numerical order. He disappeared inside the courtroom and she gamely started to go around to all of us and collect the papers.

Larry reappeared a few minutes later and lightly kidded his volunteer because she wasn't yet finished collecting the papers. Once her task was completed, the papers were dated and initialed by Larry, and redistributed back to us. At least one thing had gone well: I now had my proof of jury service for when I would return to the office. We were ready for the court, but the court was not quite ready for us. Within about fifteen minutes, we were directed into the courtroom.

We lined up in numerical order and the first twelve people were directed into the jury box. The rest of us filled up three rows of gallery bench seats at the back of the courtroom. Once we were inside and seated, Judge Douglas

Rayes introduced himself, welcomed all the prospective jurors, and administered the juror oath. Judge Rayes told us we should avoid any contact with the attorneys or anyone associated with the case. It was okay to say hello or good morning if riding on the elevator, but that was it. He was cordial and courteous and explained what would be happening that morning. We would be hearing a criminal case. The name and number of the case was read into the record and the judge explained that this trial was scheduled to last for about five weeks.

The judge asked how many jurors thought they might not be available for this trial, due to its length. Nearly every hand in the room shot up. Then the judge said that perhaps he should rephrase the question, and asked how many people would be available to serve on this trial. About six or eight hands were raised. Those individuals were instructed to go back downstairs to the jury assembly room where they would be asked to fill out a questionnaire.

For those of us remaining who indicated we could not be available, the judge then explained the lengthy trial policy. For jurors who do not receive compensation for jury service from their employers, the courts will now reimburse their pay if the trial lasts longer than ten days. This allows many more people to serve on jury duty than might otherwise be the case. One by one, each of the prospective jurors was questioned about availability to serve on this jury.

Several people were full-time college students just starting fall semester. They would be missing their classes right at the beginning of the semester. There were several teachers who similarly would be starting a new school year and it would be very difficult for a long-term substitute to take over their classes. In addition to the students and teachers within our group, there were a number of people who were caregivers for someone in the family. One person drove a family member to dialysis every other day, and would have a difficult time being available for court. As I listened to the reasons each person gave, it became painfully clear my concerns about this trial being inconvenient for my job would not be impressive to the judge. Other people had medical issues they felt would not allow them to sit for jury duty. These ranged from recent open-heart surgery to knee surgery to sleep apnea.

Judge Rayes did not automatically accept each person's reasons at face value. He had undoubtedly heard every version of "the dog ate my homework" stories from jurors over the years, and asked pointed follow-up questions to determine if substance was behind the excuses being offered. The person who had knee surgery was asked if it would help that the court took a break at least once an hour. A number of the prospective jurors explained that they had employment commitments which would make it difficult for them to serve on the jury. On closer examination, many of their commitments didn't seem as urgent as initially presented. When some expressed concern about the loss of pay, the judge patiently reviewed the lengthy trial policy and asked if this wouldn't allow them to recoup their pay and be available for jury duty. And so it went around the room, listening to the stories of about forty people who had other things they would rather do than serve on this trial as a juror.

As I sat waiting for my turn, I looked around at the other people already in the courtroom. The clerk and recorder were seated on either side of the judge's bench. Directly in front of the gallery were two tables. Three men were seated on the left, at the table directly in front of me; two men were seated at the table on the right—the side of the room where the jury box was located. In my prior jury service, the table closest to the jury was the prosecution. There were also two deputies seated to the left of the table in front of me. Not too much of a mystery there: this was the defense table.

When we entered the room, the men at both tables stood up and turned around to watch the prospective jurors enter. Once seated, we all faced the judge. The man I was sitting behind appeared be the defendant, accompanied by his attorneys. He was wearing a blue shirt and sported a very recent and short haircut.

When my turn came around, I was thankful I had my appointment calendar with me. I never dreamed there could be another five-week case in my life. It's said that lightning never strikes twice, but it looked like it could for me, if I didn't have a good reason not to be involved in this trial. When asked about my availability to serve as a juror, I explained that I had to be in Tucson on Wednesday. The judge assured me that would not be a problem. I then explained that I had a commitment the following Monday afternoon and couldn't be available that day. The judge told me that specific Monday would not be a problem either.

With a sinking feeling I mentioned my vacation plans for the last week of September. I explained that even though the trial was scheduled to be five weeks, I had served on a jury in which the trial went longer than scheduled. I had travel plans for the last week of September, and already had my reservations. The judge assured me that my travel plans wouldn't be a problem.

That was it. That was my last holdout for my lack of availability. The round of questioning moved on to the next prospect and when it was all over, another small group—myself included—was sent back to the jury assembly room to fill out that questionnaire. I could not believe this was happening. How was it possible that I could be in a panel for jury duty in another long trial?

When I returned to the jury assembly area, I was directed to a room off to the side in which other people from my panel were nearly finished filling out the questionnaire. It was a rather lengthy form, perhaps fifteen pages. Judge Rayes had instructed us that we should avoid the news because it was possible this case might be covered in the news media. I decided I'd better ask our bailiff if he could tell me what the case was about. He told me the questionnaire had information on the case, so I started reading it.

The case was simply stated in a short paragraph. A man by the name of Rick Chance was murdered at a Tempe hotel approximately three years previous. The defendant, Robert Lemke, was accused of the crime; another person, Brandi Hungerford, had been involved with the crime and was expected to testify.

Even though it had been three years, and even though I don't watch the news that much, I remembered this case. At the time, a picture from the hotel's surveillance video was aired on local news stations, showing the victim and Brandi Hungerford. As I read on, I also learned that this was a capital murder case. This was far more than I had bargained for. When you get your jury duty summons, you just don't think of the prospect that you might be selected to consider an actual life-and-death decision involving murder and the death penalty. But there it all was, neatly summarized on this questionnaire. And getting back to the questionnaire, I knew I'd better sit down and start trying to complete it.

My first inclination was to think about getting back to the office, but I knew I couldn't just blow off the questions. I had to give my answers some thought. Those answers were going to determine whether or not I became a juror in this case. The questionnaire began with questions such as educational attainment, including any special training acquired. And of course employment or job title, and the usual background information. Then another page or two later, some of the questions were repeated. Once again, educational attainment, classes taken in addition to regular education, and so forth. The instructions clearly asked for detailed answers, yet I thought about just writing "see previous question." After all, if they didn't like my answers, they might not want me as a juror and that couldn't be all bad.

Then the questions became a little more difficult. Questions about my thoughts on capital punishment. Questions about my ability to be objective as a juror. Questions about whether or not I would be willing to decide the case based on the evidence presented, and whether or not I would be willing to follow directions that were provided by the court. All of these questions had to be answered, and answered truthfully. I read each question carefully and gave the best answer I could, but tended to put down short answers. If they wanted more information, they could certainly ask about it in court.

And of course, that was exactly what would happen. After completing the questionnaire, I returned it to the bailiff and he started to write on my juror affidavit sheet the date that I would have to return for the voir dire process. I reminded him that I could not be available Wednesday because I realized everyone in my group had been scheduled to return on a Wednesday. Not a problem. He marked Thursday's date on my form. I was to return Thursday at 10:45 a.m.

That was it for now. It was time to return to the office. I mentally reviewed the questions I had just answered, and it occurred to me that there had been no questions about previous trial experience, no questions about whether or not I had ever served on a jury, or whether the jury had reached a verdict, or what that verdict might have been. In short, there had been absolutely no reference to my "ace in the hole" question I had hoped would help me avoid jury duty. But then I reasoned that perhaps when I returned Thursday, there might be additional questions—the kind that are asked in open court to a whole panel of prospective jurors. Maybe that was when I could use my "ace in the hole" question. Then I could explain that I had served on a jury before, and I could provide the information that I was so hopeful would let me avoid having to sit as a juror on this trial.

Voir Dire

Three days later, I was back in court. There were several other people waiting outside the courtroom. My assigned time was 10:45 and I went up to the entry doors to read the posted notice. At first I didn't see anything about my case and wondered if I should check the other courtrooms. Nothing was going on so I looked around for a place to wait. I sat next to another lady about my age and she asked if I was here for the voir dire. I said yes. She must have noticed me checking out the posted notice and assured me I was in the right place. Her name was Abby and on Tuesday she had been assigned to a jury panel.

Soon our bailiff Larry arrived and explained that we would be going into court one at a time in the order of our juror numbers. He returned our completed questionnaires to each of us and asked that we review our responses. When we went into court, the attorneys would ask us any additional questions they might have about our responses. I was first. Just me, not the whole panel. This was going to be each person, one at a time.

Larry escorted me into the courtroom and directed me to a chair located right in front of the jury box. I looked around the courtroom to see the judge, the clerk and recorder, two men at the prosecution table, two men sitting on the defendant's right and a woman sitting on his left at the defense table, along with a deputy sitting in the corner behind them. I wondered if the woman was a jury selection consultant for the defense. All eyes were on me. The judge welcomed me back to court and asked the attorneys if they had any questions.

The prosecuting attorney referred to a question about how I would vote if on the ballot there were a referendum regarding the death penalty. My written response stated that it would depend on the specifics in the proposal. I explained that I had some issues with the referendum process and did not like initiatives that were written in a "one size fits all" manner.

The defense attorney asked me if I would always choose the death penalty as a sentence. I said that I was not really familiar with the process on how the death penalty is determined. The attorney explained that in a sense, his questions were in reverse order because he needed to ask about the death penalty even before his client was tried on the facts of the case. He explained that this was necessary because the prosecution had requested the death penalty in this case. I said that even though I was not familiar with the process, I would be willing to follow the directions of the court.

The attorneys had no further questions and I was excused. Larry escorted me out of the courtroom, collected my questionnaire and gave me another attendance slip, asking me to return the following Wednesday at 10:45 a.m. I was in and out in a matter of minutes and no one had asked any questions about prior jury service. Things were not looking good.

Final Selection

Wednesday, August 24, 2005

The intervening week passed fairly quickly. I had an enjoyable weekend and didn't think too much about the prospect of the trial. Wednesday came around soon enough, however, and it was time for me to return to court. I decided to go to the office first, then go from the office to court. About an hour before I was due in court, I realized I had forgotten my juror badge. Unbelievable. I could either show up in court without it or run home, pick up the badge where I knew I'd left it and return to court. The time would be pretty tight. No doubt still in denial, I decided to go home, grab the juror badge and return to court. Amazingly, I made the round-trip within the allotted time and didn't break too many speeding records en route. I parked in the jurors' parking garage two blocks away and jogged most of the distance to the courthouse in my heels. I was in the court building by 10:45 and up to the 11th floor shortly thereafter.

Sure enough, I arrived under the wire. All the other prospective jurors were milling around outside the courtroom. This time it was a pretty large group and mostly unfamiliar faces. Only a few of my original group of fifty had been available for trial, so it seemed logical that there must have been other groups of fifty that were also part of this panel. I strolled up and down the corridor and took an unofficial head count. People were also there for Family Court, but they were pretty easy to spot. My unofficial estimate was around forty-five or fifty people that were likely a part of our remaining panel. That made sense, and was approximately the number of prospective jurors the courtroom could hold.

Standing along the corridor just to the left of the entrance to the courtroom, I struck up a conversation with a couple of other juror prospects. I had already met one of them, juror twenty-eight, and would be lining up behind him when we entered the courtroom. We talked about prior jury experience. He had been on a murder trial once before. I wondered if he would be selected this

11

time, since he had been on the same type of case. I shared some information about the federal court case I'd been on more than a decade ago. It was a fairly interesting case, and both men seemed receptive to idle conversation, so I continued.

The second man asked if I remembered the name of the judge in that trial. I told him no, but I thought I might recognize it if I heard the name. He gave the name of a judge and amazingly it was the judge who presided over the trial for my previous jury experience. What were the odds of that coincidence? The man explained that at the time he had been an attorney who tried many cases in federal court, and he recalled that this particular judge had tried cases of the type I described. That removed some of the mystery, but it was still a pretty amazing coincidence. He explained that he was now a judge from Avondale. I wondered if he would be picked as a juror for this case. It didn't seem likely. He explained that he felt it was ethically important to be there, because as a judge he asked people to do the same thing he was now being asked to do. His number was greater than two hundred. My number was twenty-nine.

I am convinced that the lower the juror number, the greater the likelihood of being selected for the jury. The courts use a random selection process in order to guarantee a jury of peers. If the court were picking and choosing people because they live in a specific zip code, or for any other reason, it no longer has a jury of peers. According to my theory of how the process works, the first twelve people are the jury. When one of these people is eliminated—either because they are unavailable or due to a challenge for cause or a peremptory challenge—the person with the next lowest number replaces them. I remembered the questionnaire I had filled in the previous week and I knew how a large number of people were going to answer those questions. Many would identify philosophical or religious reasons that would not allow them to sit on this case, or some past experience or other reason would eliminate an unknown number of prospects. Many people would be self-eliminated from sitting as jurors on this trial. Twenty-nine was a very low number.

11:00 a.m.

After about fifteen minutes, our bailiff asked us to line up in numerical order and file into the courtroom. As before, everyone was there: the judge, the clerk and recorder, the defense and prosecution. The judge welcomed us into the courtroom and explained that we all were qualified jurors. He once again expressed appreciation on behalf of the court for our willingness to serve. I doubted many in the room truly felt willing to do so. The judge also directed us to not watch television news during the course of the trial and to avoid reading news articles about the trial. Almost immediately, we were told there would be a short recess. As we started filing back out of the courtroom, one of the first men out the door was given some quick instructions by our bailiff, Larry. The man called to some of the jurors who were heading for the elevators and asked them to stop and wait for Larry, who was still in the courtroom. Everyone gathered around when our bailiff reappeared. Larry informed us that this recess was not something he had anticipated, and it would be fairly short—only about twenty minutes. We could go back to the jury assembly room and have a soft drink. Or perhaps smokers could have a quick smoke and return.

I wandered back down to the jury assembly room, which was now quiet and mostly deserted. I walked over to a table near the back of the room where two jigsaw puzzles were partially completed. I decided this would be the most productive use of my time at the moment; it would help quell my anxiety as I looked over the puzzle pieces. Those who worked the puzzle previously had started in typical fashion to complete the border first. I found myself looking for pieces that had a straight side, but none were to be found. I realized a few of them were missing. Little did I know that this puzzle would foreshadow the trial I was about to become a part of. It was time to go back upstairs.

12:00 noon

Recognizing that my last opportunity to avoid selection had passed, I found Larry and again reminded him of my unavailability the last week of September. He said "don't worry, we'll take good care of you." That was not what I wanted to hear, but it was better than nothing. Recess was over and we once again lined up and filed into the bench seats at the back of the courtroom. Larry directed me to an aisle seat, which would be convenient if I were selected. In the jury box, on each chair was a steno pad and a ballpoint pen. The moment of selection had arrived. The judge welcomed us back, saying that as the clerk started calling off names, each juror should move up to the jury box as directed by the bailiff. Seconds later, my name was called and I headed up to find my place as juror number three. As I passed Larry on my way to the back row, he quietly whispered "don't worry, it will be fine." Easy for him to say. We jurors were sworn in by the clerk and the remaining panelists were excused. Almost immediately we recessed for lunch. I went down to the ground floor, called my office and my family, and gave them the news—then continued on to the fast food and cafeteria corner. I felt as though I had just left the safety of a platform to take a seat on a rollercoaster with an unknown destination.

1:30 p.m.

When I returned from lunch, I stood by the security doors and waited as instructed to gain entry to the judicial offices and jury room. From now on, we would congregate in the jury room and enter court from the judicial entrance. Larry met us at the doors and we proceeded to the jury room where we quietly sat and waited to go into court. A juror sitting by the door suggested we introduce ourselves and we went around the room giving our first names. I knew I was never going to remember fifteen names right off the bat, so suggested that we give our names again, in jury number order. Everyone thought this was a good idea, so we repeated the introductions. I didn't want to draw attention when it was time to select a foreperson, but it was early and no one would remember my small suggestion anyway.

We all chatted for a while and Betty said it was going to be her birthday in a few days. She said she was the one in her office who was always in charge of birthday celebrations. We learned Mike worked for an auto glass company installing windshields. That seemed like quite the coincidence, because the victim, Rick Chance, had owned an auto glass company. The victim was known locally because he had been the spokesman for his company's television commercials. Larry entered the room and briefly joined the conversation. Then he asked us to line up in reverse order. We would file in and take our seats starting with juror number sixteen sitting at the far end of the front row, and ending with juror number one at the near end of the back row. It was time for the trial to begin.

Part 2

The Trial

Opening Statements

We entered the courtroom, found our seats, and the first order of business was our juror instructions. They were read aloud by the judge as we followed along with our own copy. The trial would consist of three phases. The first was the guilt phase and our job was to listen to all the evidence and decide whether the defendant was guilty or not guilty. If we found the defendant guilty, the second phase would be the determination of aggravation, a factor used to sentence the defendant. The third phase would be mitigation, an opportunity to consider leniency in the sentencing.

The trial would be sufficiently difficult for the jury, and the sentencing phases would only add to the complexity and difficulty of the job at hand. I had a vague recollection that some changes had occurred in sentencing procedures in recent years, and wondered if our instructions were impacted by those changes. I realized I knew nothing about the death penalty, yet was already learning far more than I wanted to know about capital punishment in Arizona.

The attorneys moved right into opening statements. The prosecuting attorney, Sam Myers, described a cast of characters involved in a series of events leading to the robbery and murder of the victim, Rick Chance. The defendant, Robert Lemke, and his accomplice, Brandi Hungerford, made use of a classified ad for Rolex watches to meet and eventually rob the victim.

It was Brandi who made contact. "Plan A" was for Brandi to gain an invitation to the victim's house, put a sleeping pill in his drink, and when he passed out Robert would enter the scene, tie up the victim with duct tape and rob him of the jewelry in his home. This plan was unsuccessful, so "Plan B" was essentially the same but at a hotel instead of the victim's house. The prosecution would prove that "Plan B" took place, resulting in the robbery

15

and murder of Rick Chance, and that after the crime both Brandi and Robert went to Robert's friend with a gun in a pizza box and asked the friend to sell it. Then the next day, Brandi and Robert fled to Tacoma. After their arrival in Washington, the police apprehended Robert, at which time he attempted to run. Brandi was arrested the following day.

The defense attorney, Bruce Peterson, agreed that a terrible crime had been committed and that Mr. Chance had tragically lost his life in the commission of that crime. However, the defense asked the jury to concentrate on the testimony of each witness as it pertained to instruction number eight, Credibility of Witnesses. The defense attorney assured us we would see the guilty party in the courtroom, but that it was not his client, the defendant.

The Prosecution's Case

Witness One: Fred Pratt,
General Manager of the hotel where the crime was committed.

The hotel was a four-story building with one-hundred-three rooms located near Scottsdale Road and the Loop 202. The hotel had eight surveillance cameras outside the building at various entrances. There were also surveillance cameras at the registration area, and the third floor vending room. Each camera recorded a few seconds of activity on a disk in a sequential rotation. The night of the crime, the victim and his companion checked into the hotel at about 9:16 p.m. Hotel records indicated that the key card had been used once, about 9:19 p.m. The room status for housekeeping was "occupied and dirty." Shortly after checkout time the following afternoon, a maid opened the door to the room and discovered the body of the murder victim. She contacted the manager and the police were called immediately.

Witness Two: Detective Trent Luckow

Detective Luckow reviewed the surveillance videos and prepared still photos from the video. Exhibit thirty-nine, the videotape, was used to produce Exhibit fifty-two, a photo of the victim and Brandi checking in at the registration desk of the hotel. Exhibit fifty-three was a photo of the victim and Brandi leaving the hotel lobby and walking through the circular entry drive back toward the parking area. Exhibit fifty-one was a photo from the third floor vending room showing a female subject with her back to the vending machines and camera. Exhibit fifty showed a male subject walking along the corridor in front of the entrance to the third floor vending room. The detective explained that when he checked out the surveillance system, the time stamp on all of the video photos was approximately twenty minutes fast, as compared to his watch.

Witness Three: Dr. Phillip Keen, Chief Medical Examiner

Dr. Keen explained that he had been contacted by the police to examine the victim at the crime scene. He was initially able to determine the cause of death as a gunshot wound, and the manner of death was murder. The autopsy was performed on the Saturday following the murder. The victim was a male, seventy-five inches tall, or six-foot-three-inches, weighing two-hundred-forty-five pounds. An x-ray revealed a bullet in the chest. The right ear had a laceration, which is a blunt-force tear, commonly known as a "cut." There was also bruising of the scalp behind the ear on the right side. A closely-cropped enlargement of a photograph showed the bruising formed two parallel lines. The injury was more likely to have been caused by the victim being struck by an object such as the barrel of a pistol, rather than the victim's head striking something such as a table. There was another bruised area on the left side of the scalp.

The gunpowder spread indicated the victim was shot from a distance of six to thirty inches. The Medical Examiner showed a diagram of the body to illustrate the path of the bullet. Rick Chance had been shot once from above his right shoulder. The victim also had an abrasion on his nose and another on his left hand, where it appeared a ring was missing. The examiner also noted that the victim had a prosthesis for his right eye.

Dr. Keen outlined the order of injuries. The parietal blow to the scalp and ear laceration preceded the gunshot wound, because there was evidence of bleeding. The blow to the left side of the scalp also occurred prior to the gunshot wound, for the same reason. The timing of the abrasion to the nose and finger was unknown since no bleeding occurred. The bullet entered from the side and above, which could be determined by the abrasion cuff of the wound. The entry was about the third or fourth rib and the path continued through the right lung, piercing the aorta, through the left lung, and coming to

17

rest near the eighth rib in back. Death occurred within minutes or perhaps less than a minute. The victim may have been sitting or lying down when shot from an attitude above and to the right. The assailant could have been a small or large person. After the attorneys questioned each witness, jurors were allowed to ask questions by raising a hand and submitting the question in writing. The judge and attorneys would review the question, and if approved, it would be directed to the witness. One of the jurors asked about the force required to inflict the injuries to the victim's head. Dr. Keen responded that just the inertia from swinging the weapon would be sufficient. Court recessed around 4:00 p.m., and our first day of the trial was over.

Thursday, August 25, 2005 — 2:00 p.m.

Witness Four: Brandi Hungerford

Direct Examination

Brandi stated she was twenty-eight years old, five-foot-three-inches in height and weighed approximately 138 pounds. In 2002 she had weighed about 125 pounds. She reviewed her plea agreement. On August 27th, she pled guilty to second degree murder, armed robbery, and conspiracy to commit armed robbery. She agreed to these charges on the condition that she testify at the trial of Robert Lemke. Her agreement required that she tell the truth about the events that took place in 2002, concerning the robbery and murder of Rick Chance.

Brandi met Robert Lemke in 2002, perhaps six months prior to August. Initially their relationship was that of boyfriend/girlfriend, but later changed to just friends. They did not live together but often stayed together, either at the Tempe apartment of Robert's friend Mary, or at Robert's house in Cave Creek where he had a roommate named Gillian. At that time, Brandi was working but Robert was not. He had a nickname of "Dakota." She did not have a gun, but Robert did.

Brandi met Rick Chance about June of 2002. She had called on a classified ad for jewelry. Robert told her to set up a meeting to purchase watches from Chance. She met with Rick Chance the same day, at Starbucks. She called herself "Kim." Rick Chance showed her some watches and she expressed potential interest, saying she would think about it. He gave her his business card and on the back wrote the name and number of a California jewelry dealer. Brandi had a cell phone she used, set up in the name and social security number of someone named Pam. She received information from Robert to set up the account.

The second meeting with Rick Chance was at the Tequila Grill, perhaps a week later. Robert wanted the robbery to take place at Chance's house. Brandi would drug Chance, and Robert would tie up and rob him.

Brandi did not have a car. She had totaled her own car driving back from New Mexico, where she hit an animal on the road. That might have occurred about April, but Brandi couldn't remember. She drove Robert's Cadillac and followed Rick Chance to his house. She called Robert by cell phone once en route to the house and a second time from the bathroom of the victim's house.

Once at the house, Robert told her to look for jewelry. The only jewelry she observed was the watch, ring and bracelet Rick Chance was wearing. He changed clothing in the bathroom. She put the contents of a sleeping capsule in his drink, but instead of passing out, he felt tired after drinking about half the drink, decided to end the evening, and walked Brandi to her car.

Brandi learned that Rick Chance's children would be coming and staying with him at his house, so Robert decided they should arrange the next encounter at a hotel located near the freeway, in Tempe. Brandi knew of the Denny's coffee shop located next to the hotel, and Robert checked out the surveillance. The hotel had cameras, but Robert didn't think they worked. Brandi testified that she had been a willing participant in the plan because she anticipated splitting half of the money from the robbery, and she needed a car.

The third meeting with Rick Chance was at Bandera's in Scottsdale. The plan was just to have dinner and let Chance take the lead in the conversation. The two walked around after dinner, and as a prank they taped a blown-up condom to a statue. During the evening, Brandi told Chance she had a friend who was interested in buying a watch and jewelry for his girlfriend.

The fourth meeting with Rick Chance took place on the evening of August 8. Brandi met Rick at P. F. Chang's for dinner. Robert dropped her off at the restaurant at around 8:30. After dinner, Rick Chance drove with Brandi to the hotel Brandi and Robert had found. Chance wore a watch and a ring and had a black bag with jewelry. Brandi told Chance that the friend interested in buying jewelry would meet them at the coffee shop next door to the hotel. About the time they arrived at the hotel, Brandi called Robert on her cell phone from Rick Chance's car. Robert was about ten or fifteen minutes away from the hotel, at Mary's apartment. Rick and Brandi checked into the hotel together, returned to Rick's car, then went up to their room on the third floor.

Once inside the hotel guest room, Brandi waited for Robert to get to the hotel. From the bathroom, she again called him on her cell phone. He asked if she were on the first floor, second floor, and so on. He skipped to the fourth floor and Brandi said she would see him in three minutes. He then asked if she were on the third floor and she said yes. She waited a few more minutes and then left the room. In order to keep Rick in the room, she told him to start undressing. Heading out of the room toward the elevators and vending room to the left, she saw Robert at the other end of the hallway. He was wearing black pants and a dress shirt.

Brandi met up with Robert in the sitting area by the elevators. Robert was carrying a blue plastic bag with a yellow smiley face, similar to one she had seen at the apartment. The bag contained duct tape, a ski mask, and a gun. She told Robert she had left the door to the room ajar, and directed him to the second set of doors down the hallway. She went toward the vending room and saw Robert with the ski mask and red gloves on as he entered Chance's room, his arms straight out in front of him, holding the gun. She heard a loud noise that scared her; she wanted to go hide. She came out of the vending room, went down to the car, and waited for Robert. Within a minute or so, Robert returned to the car. The next day, she saw Robert throw the blue sack into a dumpster.

Brandi said they returned to the apartment in Tempe, where Robert looked through the contents of the black bag and clipped the price tags off the jewelry. Brandi picked up the tags from the floor and put them in the trash. There were six watches which she had seen from her visit with Rick Chance at Starbucks, as well as earrings and pendants. They later drove in Robert's Cadillac to the house of Robert's friend Dan. They brought the black gym bag with the jewelry, and they also brought a pizza box with a gun inside. Brandi said Robert asked Dan to hold it for him. After that, they left and drove in Robert's car to his house in Cave Creek, where they stayed the night.

The next day they returned to Mary's apartment for an hour or two. Robert wanted to drive to Tacoma. He called Mary, asking if he could drive her Pathfinder. It was her brother's; Mary asked that it be taken back to Tacoma.

Brandi said the real purpose of the trip was to sell the jewelry. They drove straight through to Tacoma, stopping only at gas stations to make calls and at a restaurant to use the restroom. When they arrived in Tacoma, they met Robert's sister and mother at his mother's apartment. Brandi took a nap after they arrived. Later they went to a hotel with Robert's sister and the sister's boyfriend. They stayed at the hotel about two days. A friend of Robert's bought one of the watches for $4,000. Brandi counted the money for the transaction.

After two days, they went to Brad's loft. Brad was a friend of Robert's and they stayed with him for about two days. After that, Robert was picked up by the police. Brandi stayed with Peggy, Robert's mother. The Tacoma police also came to Peggy's apartment and picked up Brandi for questioning. Brandi said she denied any knowledge of the robbery when first questioned. She also said she was told Rick Chance was dead, but at first she didn't believe it. She said that at later interviews with both Tempe and Tacoma police present, she told the truth.

Cross Examination

During cross-examination, Brandi said she had worked at Christie's Cabaret for approximately four years. The attorney asked her if she hated Rick Chance and she said she hated guys who try to buy women. The attorney asked her what Robert was wearing at the hotel when the robbery took place. Brandi said he wore black dress pants; that he was dressed up. The attorney asked if he had a collared shirt; she said he was not wearing a casual shirt. The attorney asked Brandi if she had ever fired a handgun. She said yes, she had fired a Glock.

At the time of her arrest, Brandi gave two recorded interviews to the Tempe police. One was on Thursday, August 15; the second was on Friday, August 16. Brandi's first interview occurred on Wednesday, August 14, with the Tacoma police. It was not recorded.

The defense attorney also interviewed Brandi in July 2005, just prior to the trial. The attorney asked her what she saw in the hotel, and whether or not she saw Robert holding a gun. He referred to her testimony of August 15, in which she stated he was holding his arms "like he was holding a gun." but she also said she couldn't see the gun because his arms were already past the doorframe and out of her view. The attorney referred to her testimony on the witness stand in which she said she had seen the gun, because she described Robert as holding the gun, with his arms straight out in front of him.

The defense attorney and the prosecuting attorney went to the bench for a sidebar conference. The judge then announced that it was time to recess for the day. It was shortly after 4:30 p.m.

The first short week of testimony ended, and we had only been at trial on Wednesday and Thursday afternoon. I went to work on Friday and then the weekend arrived. I spent a great deal of time thinking about all the testimony that had already been presented. I thought about what had happened to the murder victim. I wondered what the specific events were that took place inside that hotel room. It seemed clear that no one would ever know for sure what had happened, because the only two people present were Rick Chance and the assailant. Rick Chance had died and the assailant would never volunteer any information about what really happened.

Monday, August 29, 2005 — 1:30 p.m.

All the jurors arrived on Monday, ready to continue with the trial. We did not convene until 1:30 p.m., so this would be another half day of testimony. I arrived at the courthouse and managed to pass through the security inspection and make my way up to the jury room with no delays. I sat in the far corner of the room next to Pete, who worked for a trucking company. We talked a little about our experience in the voir dire process and when asked about whether he'd remembered hearing about the murder at the time, he had told the attorneys that he and his coworkers had joked about the circumstances, as guys will do. Pete was tall and solidly built and about the size of the victim. I was an inch or two taller than Brandi but about the same weight. I had a difficult time picturing myself getting close enough to someone Pete's size to hit him with a handgun. I thought to myself that such a tactic could go horribly wrong from the woman's perspective.

We were expecting to hear the continuation of cross-examination of Brandi Hungerford by the defense attorney. However when we filed into the courtroom, there was no sign of Brandi.

Witness 5: Mary, friend of Robert

Mary was originally from Washington State and had lived in Arizona for three and a half years. In 1996 she met Robert in high school. In 1999, she dated Robert's best friend and roommate, David. Mary had been a student at ASU and during the summer of 2002 she asked Robert to house-sit her apartment while she returned to Tacoma. She also met Brandi through Robert. Mary said she had a Nissan Pathfinder, which actually belonged to her parents. Robert called her to ask if he could drive up in the Pathfinder, switch cars in Tacoma, and bring down her Honda Civic. He called a couple of days in advance. Robert had also asked if he could borrow $200 for the trip, to which Mary agreed. She met Brandi, Robert, and Robert's sister, and stayed with them at their hotel that night until about noon the next day. They all sat and watched movies. The next day they went over to the loft of Robert's friend, Brad.

Under cross-examination, the defense attorney asked Mary if Brandi and Robert got along, or if they fought. Mary replied that while she was with them at the hotel, sometimes Brandi and Robert argued. They all just hung out there, watched movies and fell asleep. There was no discussion regarding jewelry. The defense asked about her friendship with Robert and she said Robert was like a big brother. He had helped her with her apartment and in getting a bed. When questioned further, she also said Robert was not controlling of Brandi. Mary said Robert took about $500 rather than the $200 he asked to borrow for the trip, and that had been okay with her. Her entire testimony lasted about twenty minutes, followed by a short afternoon recess.

2:10 p.m.

Witness 6: Brad, friend of Robert

Brad lived in an apartment loft on Pacific Avenue in Tacoma. He met Robert—or 'Robbie'—a month or two after moving to Tacoma, around 1998 or 1999. Robert had called him and said he would be in town, and wanted to come over and stay with Brad. He thought Robert initially called him on a Thursday. However, on Friday, Brad had flown to Oakland to visit a friend and didn't return until after the weekend. Brad recalled that he probably did not see Robert until Monday. Robert was with Brandi, whom Brad had met about a month earlier. Brandi and Robert stayed with Brad on Monday, Tuesday and Wednesday. They didn't have a car. He noticed there was some tension between Brandi and Robert, and thought it had to do with Brandi's ex-boyfriend. Brandi was upset and Brad offered to take her to have her nails done. Robert told Brad not to take Brandi out and said don't let her use the phone. Robert said she was trying to get in touch with her ex-boyfriend.

Robert showed Brad a white gold and diamond watch. Robert told him that a kid he knew had given it to him to pay off a debt. Robert was trying to get rid of the watch and wanted to sell it.

Brad agreed to give Robert a ride to the rental car company because Robert wanted to rent a car. Brad was driving and Robert was a passenger when they were stopped by the police approximately one mile from the apartment. Brad said there were about twenty police all over the place who gave them orders over a megaphone. Brad was taken into custody and later released. Once he returned home, he noticed a bag of dog food in the corridor, a pillow, and a bag he did not recognize, which he delivered to the police.

Brad was asked if he recognized Exhibit 36, a business card that belonged to Rick Chance. He did not recognize it. He was also asked if he recognized a black bag, Exhibit 46. He did not. A juror asked a question about the car rental.

Under cross-examination, the defense attorney asked about Brandi's demeanor. Brad said this was only the second time he had been around her, but that sometimes she was kind of a bitch. Brad also said he had overheard an argument in which she told Robert she hated him. Brad said Robert had her penned up in his apartment.

Witness 7: Detective Tom Magazzini, Tempe Police Department

Detective Magazzini arrived at the scene of the crime at the hotel around 2 p.m. on Friday August 9. The crime scene had been secured, including the hotel room and an adjacent hallway. The door was ajar. There was a spent shell case near the door, and a body near the bed. Exhibit 54 was a diagram of the crime scene. The victim was lying face down on his left side. A ring was on his right hand, and a cigar between his face and the floor. The jury was shown photographs of the bed. One photo, Exhibit 3, showed blood on the bedspread at the far corner of the foot of the bed. The other photo, Exhibit 4, showed blood on the far side and edge of the bedspread, about midway between the head and foot of the bed. On the desk were two key cards and an orange pill; two baggies were wedged in a chair cushion. There were also two tissues in the wastebasket under the sink in the bathroom. Two juror questions were submitted. Only one question was asked about whether the victim could have been sitting on the bed.

Under cross-examination, the defense attorney asked about the location of the elevators in relation to the room. The hotel room was east of the elevators. The vending room was on the south side of a hallway, west of the elevators. The defense attorney also asked about the ring on the victim's hand. The detective described the ring as having a stone the size of a dime. In the victim's right front pants pocket was a money clip with $2,381 and two condoms. The attorney also asked about the shell casing. It was described as a nine millimeter shell designed for use in a semi-automatic weapon.

Witness 8: Detective John Ferrin, Tempe Police Department

Detective Ferrin was the case agent or lead investigator for this case. Throughout the trial he sat at the prosecution table with Mr. Myers. Detective Ferrin recovered the bullet from the autopsy that took place on Saturday, and was also involved in the search of Mary's apartment in Tempe. Exhibit 28 was the bullet; Exhibit 30 was three jewelry tags used by Rick Chance and Exhibit 37 was the same kind of jewelry tags taken from the apartment.

At the completion of Detective Ferrin's testimony, we were through hearing testimony for the day. Although only 4:15 p.m., it had been a long afternoon.

On Monday evening I found myself standing in my own bedroom looking at the relationship of the bed and other furniture in my room, and mentally trying to match it up with the murder scene. I moved about the room and wondered where the victim might have been standing, and whether the assailant came from behind and surprised the victim, or whether they confronted one another.

The victim was found lying on his side, face down at the foot of the bed. I thought about the pistol and what direction the spent shell would go when ejected from it. It had landed somewhere between the victim and the door to the room. But then I didn't know anything about where either the assailant or victim might have been standing, or at what angle the gun might have been held. The defense attorney had suggested that the shell casing might have bounced when it was ejected, or it might have been kicked by someone, or any number of other scenarios. Obviously, sitting on the jury of a murder trial was nothing like watching a murder mystery on television, where the scene is played out at the beginning and then during the course of the next hour the characters determine with certainty what occurred. All I knew was that we had covered a great deal of territory in a very short time.

Tuesday, August 30, 2005 — 10:45 a.m.

Witness 9: Detective Brian Vold, Tacoma Police Department

On August 13, Detective Vold had been contacted by Detective Tom O'Brien and conducted surveillance at Brad's apartment. On August 14 at 1:56 p.m., two white males with two dogs left the complex in a Toyota 4Runner—Brad's vehicle.

Police conducted a "high risk stop" of the vehicle. Brad followed instructions, was removed from the vehicle, and taken into custody. Robert turned toward the console and moved his hands in a downward motion, rather than keeping them up in plain sight as instructed. Robert was asked to get out of the car and lie flat on the ground. He got out of the car as instructed but did not lie down on the ground with his arms spread as instructed. Instead his arms were close to his sides. After lowering himself to the ground, suddenly he sprang up at least a foot off the ground and took off running. The detective had never seen anything quite like it. Within 100-150 feet, upon reaching a chain link fence, he was tackled.

Under cross-examination, the defense asked Detective Vold if he was present when Detective Baker interviewed Brandi Hungerford, and whether she was uncooperative. He responded that Detective Baker interviewed Brandi and that she became less cooperative.

Witness 10: Detective Ed Baker, Tacoma Police Department

Detective Baker went to the apartment to do a welfare check on Brandi Hungerford. She was taken to the police station for interview, which was completed around 5:30 or 6:00. At that time she requested that she be taken to Robert's mother's apartment. The next day the Tempe police interviewed Brandi. Detective Baker also assisted with obtaining blood samples from Robert Lemke and Brandi Hungerford, as well as assisting with obtaining telephone recordings from the county jail.

The defense attorney asked about the original interview with Brandi that was not recorded. That interview started at approximately 2:30 p.m. and at the request of Brandi was ended at 6:05 p.m. The detective had gone to get her. She was alone in the apartment and in a robe. It appeared that she had just showered or recently awoken. When asked by the defense attorney about the high-risk felony stop, the detective said he saw no furtive movements, but he also said he did not have a view of the passenger side of the vehicle. When asked about Brandi's demeanor, the detective stated that his early observation of her behavior was that she was forthcoming. However, after the Tempe detective gave her certain information, her demeanor changed and her answers became short. The interview was terminated at 6:05 p.m. when Brandi asked to be taken back to the apartment.

Witness 8 (recalled): Detective John Ferrin, Tempe Police Department

Detective Ferrin was involved in the search of Mary's apartment and Robert's Cave Creek house. In the Tempe apartment, a Rolex watch was found in a kitchen cabinet above the microwave. At the Cave Creek house, a Rolex was found in the master bathroom. There was also a torn-up note in the trash in front of the Cave Creek House.

Detective Ferrin was also involved in the search of Brad's apartment in Tacoma. A Geneva watch was found in a piece of luggage and a Chopard watch was found on the top shelf of the closet in the bedroom where Robert had been staying. The luggage also had Robert's driver's license. Exhibit 58 was a photo of the Chopard watch. Money was also found in the Tacoma apartment: $2,400 was found inside a book of poems, $4,050 was found in a sock drawer, and $20,020 was found in the closet in a black fur hat.

In the search of the Toyota 4Runner, items were found between the seat and the console. One of the items was a business card for C. Richard Chance. The detective was asked to examine the card and he said there were no markings on the back except a squiggle that he could not read. A little later, he looked at the back of the card again and realized that when turned right side up, the squiggle was where he had initialed the card as evidence. Property was also delivered to the Police Department by Brad.

Detective Ferrin said three people were at the Tacoma Sheraton: Brandi, Robert and Robert's sister. A parking pass issued to Robert from August 10-12 was found in the Pathfinder.

Rick Chance's attorney, Candess Hunter, provided paperwork on the Chopard watch. The serial number from the receipt for the Chopard watch matched the serial number on the watch found in the Tacoma apartment.

The attorney asked about whether any fingerprints were identified. The detective reported that none of the defendant's fingerprints were found on Rick Chance's vehicle. Brandi's prints were found at the Tempe hotel. Her prints were also found on the jewelry tags at Mary's apartment. On the IDs found in the apartment, Robert was described as six feet tall and weighing 230-240 pounds.

It was another information-packed morning, even though the court was only in session for about an hour and recessed for lunch just before noon.

1:45 p.m.

Witness 11: Gillian, friend of Robert

Gillian was twenty-five years old and knew Robert three or four years. She had been a roommate at his house in Cave Creek from April or May of 2002 through August. She was contacted by police on Tuesday, August 13. The last time she saw Robert was on Thursday, August 8, when he and Brandi showed up unexpectedly that evening. Robert was wearing slacks. Brandi was wearing jeans and a beige top. The next morning, Friday, Robert knocked on her door and said, "if the cops come by, you haven't seen me." She also said that Robert had guns in the house.

Under cross-examination, the defense attorney asked about the slacks Robert was wearing. She said they were light gray. The defense attorney asked whether there was any unusual behavior and she said there was no unusual behavior. In a previous interview, Gillian said that Brandi had been pretty rude to her.

Witness 12: Detective Susan Schoville, Tempe Police Department

Detective Schoville was involved in the search of Robert's Cadillac. The search revealed a newspaper with classified ads, stuffed between the driver's seat and console. Exhibit 17 was a photograph showing the classified section tucked between the seat and console. Exhibit 45 was the actual classified section, CL5, from the May 5, 2002 edition of *The Arizona Republic*. The detective was able to identify the ad placed by Rick Chance. It was prominently positioned within the folds of the page but not circled or highlighted.

Detective Schoville was also involved in obtaining the downloaded telephone calls on CD from the Tacoma jail.

Witness 8 (recalled): Detective John Ferrin, Tempe Police Department

Under cross-examination by the defense attorney, the detective stated that it was Brandi's fingerprint on the bathroom sink in the hotel. He was also asked about a surveillance photo from the vending room, that of a male wearing dark slacks. The attorney asked the direction the male subject was going. The detective said the direction would have been west, which would be away from the room, not towards the room of Rick Chance.

The short afternoon of testimony went quickly and court recessed about 2:15 p.m. I would actually be getting to the office at a decent hour so I could get some work done before evening. On most trial days, I would at least check my email messages to make sure information kept moving as needed. Although I was missing a lot of time from work, my work responsibilities didn't go away.

Wednesday August 31, 2005 — 10:45 a.m.

Witness 13: Candess Hunter, Rick Chance's attorney.

Candess Hunter worked with Rick Chance in 1998 when he was a divorce client. On August 9 she was present with a film crew that was scheduled to shoot a commercial for the jewelry company. Rick Chance failed to show up for the film shoot and when she could not locate him, had called the Paradise Valley police. When asked about his classified ad for men's Rolex watches, she stated that she had advised Mr. Chance to use his cell phone number in the classifieds.

Exhibit 44 was a photograph of documents from Rick Chance's house provided by Candess Hunter to the Tempe Police Department. Mr. Chance kept his valuables in a safe and Candess Hunter had arranged to have a locksmith come out to drill open the safe. She also arranged to have various people present at the safe opening, including the family, someone from the jewelry company, and the Tempe Police Department. The safe contained a canvas bag with approximately $53,000 in cash, as well as bangle bracelets with tags. The price tags were for the jewelry company that Rick Chance represented.

Witness 14: Detective Todd Bailey, Tempe Police Department

Detective Bailey had executed a search warrant at the Chance residence. Jewelry tags from the safe were the same as those found in the Tempe apartment. Also the city trash barrel at the home had an inflated condom. Detective Bailey was also assigned to visit Christie's Cabaret, and other topless dance bars to interview people who knew Brandi.

Witness 15: Dan, friend of Robert

Dan was 26 years old and testified that he had been contacted on the morning of August 22 by the Tempe Police Department. He provided a firearm to the Police Department that he had possessed for a couple of weeks. He received the firearm from Robert and Brandi. He said he was a friend of Robert's. Dan said Robert carried in a pizza box that had a firearm inside the box. He couldn't remember any particulars about the firearm, only that it was a handgun. Robert and Brandi were only there for about fifteen to thirty minutes. Later, he received one call from Robert, who said he would be back. He also received a call from someone else about the firearm, but it had already been sold. Dan said that he understood from Robert that the gun was in good working order and Robert had said it was clean.

Court recessed about 11:30 a.m. It was time for lunch. Larry had announced earlier in the week that we would be going to lunch as a group, to celebrate Betty's birthday. We filed down the corridor, Larry and his assistant accessed the service elevator, all eighteen of us got into the elevator car and took an express ride to the ground floor. With Larry in the lead, we made our way across intersections, through office atriums, and past what seemed like blocks of construction. Our destination was a nearby deli, very popular with the downtown lunch crowd. We randomly lined up to order our sandwiches, then settled over at a group of tables our guides had secured. We continued to get acquainted with one another. The jury was a cross-section of both working and retirement age people. Some of us talked about Phoenix in the old days and the schools we had attended. I had attended Central High and Pete said our youngest juror was nineteen years old and had also attended Central.

Soon it was time to return and Larry led the way back through the labyrinth of construction, shortcuts through office buildings and so on. He started across an intersection at the end of the traffic light cycle and all sixteen of us followed in line, even though the light was about to change. Abby observed that we were just like goslings following the mother goose. We returned to the jury room, lined up and filed into court.

1:30 p.m.

Witness 16: Detective Larry Baggs, Tempe Police Department

On August 22, Detective Baggs met with Dan and recovered the handgun. It was then turned over to Detective Doran. The detective was asked to identify

Exhibit 27, which consisted of a 9 mm Smith and Wesson pistol, a magazine and one loose round. When it was recovered there was no ammunition in either the magazine or the chamber of the pistol. The detective also noted a phone number from Dan's pager and obtained the number. The area code was 253, the Seattle area. Two juror questions were submitted, only one was asked.

Under cross-examination, the detective was asked if an unidentified person had said they had wiped it down. Detective Baggs replied yes, that Dan had led him to another individual who was not identified. That person was in possession of the gun and referring to the firearm said that they had wiped it down. The defense attorney also asked about the August 15th interview with Brandi. Detective Baggs along with his partner, Detective Schoville went to Washington to interview Brandi. According to Detective Baggs, when they arrived, Brandi said she had been sitting around waiting for them to come.

Witness 17: Criminalist Lisa Peloza, Department of Public Safety Crime Lab

On August 27, Ms. Peloza received the pistol from the Tempe Police Department. Her assignment was to check the pistol to see if it functioned properly and also to fire evidence from the pistol. The gun was an SW9V, a Smith & Wesson 9 mm Luger. It could also fire a .380 caliber, which is equivalent to a 9 mm short. Exhibit 28, the bullet from the victim, matched the bullet Ms. Paloza fired from the pistol. Exhibit 29 was a casing from the gun that matched the murder weapon.

Under cross-examination, the defense attorney asked about the safety of the particular Smith & Wesson firearm. Ms. Peloza explained that it has a manual safety.

Witness 18: Detective John McGowan, Tempe Police Department

Detective McGowan obtained a list of all outgoing calls placed from Pierce County Jail in Tacoma by the defendant. He explained that all outgoing calls placed by inmates of the county jail are recorded and notice is given to inmates that all calls are recorded.

Detective McGowan also checked the phone records for the cell phone that was used by Brandi. On August 8th, the date of the crime, Brandi's cell phone had received an incoming call from the pay phone at Denny's coffee shop, next door to the hotel. The call was received around 9:28 p.m. and lasted for one minute and thirty-five seconds. The next previous call occurred at 9:08 p.m. and was an outgoing call to Mary's apartment. That call lasted for three minutes and thirteen seconds. The next previous call was placed earlier that same evening at 7:39 p.m. to area code 253, the Seattle area. On August 13th, the Denny's pay phone in the lobby was checked for evidence. No evidence was found.

Under cross-examination, the defense attorney asked more about the type of evidence. The detective said the evidence technician had been asked to look for biological evidence and did a swab for DNA. There were no usable fingerprints.

The defense attorney also asked if the police had checked calls Brandi made from the county jail. The detective stated that Brandi's calls had been checked for calls to the 480 and 602 area codes, as well as known numbers in the 253 area code. Her first call was on August 18, and was placed to her mother. The call lasted about twenty minutes. Her second call was placed to her ex-boyfriend but the call was not connected. Several additional calls were placed to both Brandi's mother and her ex-boyfriend Paul. She did not make contact with her ex-boyfriend until August 20.

Two juror questions were submitted and asked. The first juror question asked for a list of the phone numbers of calls placed by Robert. The detective read off the list of calls from his report. On August 17th Robert placed calls from county jail to his mother and three individuals named Cliff, Richard and Brian. The second juror question asked about the call to Robert's friend Dan. The detective answered that at 11:53 a.m. Robert attempted to contact his friend Dan. Robert repeatedly tried to call the same individuals on several occasions.

At the conclusion of Detective McGowan's testimony, at 2:45 p.m., court recessed for the day and week.

Tuesday, September 6, 2005 — 1:30 p.m.

The trial was now in its third week. The first week consisted of two packed afternoons with testimony from the hotel manager, the first Tempe detective, the Chief Medical Examiner and star witness Brandi Hungerford. The second week we had court for two and one-half days. Each day we heard from four to six witnesses. One of the jurors had travel plans, so court was not scheduled on Thursday. I took encouragement from that because I still had concerns about my travel plans for the last week of September.

The Thursday recess plus a Monday holiday gave jurors a five-day respite from attending the trial. It was a welcome break. One of the jurors, Debbie, was expecting her first child the beginning of October. Some of the jurors thought she looked bigger after the long weekend and asked if the baby was starting to drop. She said yes.

Witness 19: Criminalist Ramona Dedden, employed by Secure Technology.

Secure Technology recorded all phone calls of inmates at the Tacoma County Jail. She checked phone numbers provided by the Tempe Police Department and at their request created a CD of all identified calls.

Witness 20: David, friend of Robert

David lived in Phoenix briefly in 2002. He had been friends with Robert for about fifteen years and for a while lived with Robert in Phoenix. David purchased a new Smith & Wesson pistol which he kept in his room at Robert's house. David was interested in the gun as a collector. He had the pistol until the time he left Arizona, which was a few months after the purchase. He left the gun on the top shelf of a closet, locked in a plastic case. He did not take it with him when he returned to Washington because he flew back. Another friend, Tyler, had contacted David to say he had David's gun and was going to drive up to Washington and return it to

David. Tyler called once after that and said he had car trouble in Las Vegas. David never received the pistol.

Under cross-examination, David was asked if Robert had ever shown interest in the gun and David said Robert had expressed no interest in the gun. A juror submitted a question asking where the padlock key was. David said he didn't know.

Court generally convened about 10:30 in the morning and then recessed for lunch around 11:30 or 12 noon. We would usually return from lunch about 1:30 and continue until about 4:00 or 4:30 into the afternoon. We usually had a break midway through the morning and afternoon sessions. Whenever the jury would file into the courtroom, everyone in court was already assembled and in their places—the judge, the prosecution and defense counsel, the recorder, clerk and so forth.

We never saw Robert Lemke move from his station at the defense table. We never saw him take even one step. Brandi, on the other hand, was escorted into court wearing black and white jail stripes, complete with pink-trimmed handcuffs, the infamous Maricopa County Jail pink underwear in the form of pink socks, along with leg irons.

Brandi began her testimony on Thursday, the second day of the trial. The jury expected her to return the following Monday morning, but that did not happen. Instead, the attorneys had a sidebar at the judge's bench late Thursday afternoon, and the following Monday we heard from a new witness. Returning from our Labor Day weekend, court started in the afternoon with two witnesses and then suddenly there before us, Brandi was back on the stand.

2:00 p.m.

Witness 4 (recalled): Brandi Hungerford

Cross-Examination (continued)

Brandi took the stand and was given a thick notebook of transcripts from her previous interviews. The defense attorney directed her to a page from her interview with the Tempe police on August 16. He said that in her August 16 interview regarding the shot she heard, she had said "it was a gunfire" and that "I assumed that … he shot him." Then the defense attorney reminded Brandi that in court testimony, she said she didn't know he had been shot. He asked her if those were her words in the August 16 interview. Brandi responded that what he read was what she said in the interview.

The defense attorney referred to Brandi's interview from August 15 in which she said she had told everything she saw. He pointed out that in the August 15 interview, she never said she attempted to drug Rick Chance or that she had hung out, smoked weed or played with the cats. She just said "and that was about it." Also in the August 15th interview, she had not mentioned her special code to Robert when he called to ask what floor they were on and she had replied that she would see him in three minutes. The attorney also questioned why she didn't give Robert the room number once she saw him on the third floor.

The attorney asked Brandi how much she knew about what had happened in the hotel room. Brandi said that on the ride back to Mary's apartment she asked Robert "Did everything turn out okay" and "Did you get what you wanted?" In her August 15 interview, Brandi said Robert told her he had taped up the victim and left him in the bathroom. The defense attorney asked her additional information regarding her statements about directing Robert to the hotel guest room. The attorney pointed out that in her interview, Brandi used statements such as "I'm going to go with," or "I'm going to say."

The defense attorney questioned her about her description of Robert crouching down at the east end of the sitting area and putting on the ski mask in preparation for going into the hotel room. He also asked her when she left the vending room, where she was standing, and whether she could see Robert's whole body from her vantage point in the hallway.

The attorney pointed out that she had told the police additional details in her interview on August 16. For example, she first said she used the cell phone number from the ad to contact the victim. Later, she said at their first meeting at Starbucks, Rick Chance gave her his phone number. The defense also asked about her relationship with the victim and why she didn't go back to the room and check on him after she heard the gunshot sound. He asked her if it was because she didn't like him enough. Brandi responded yes and repeated that it was because she didn't like him enough. She also stated that she wasn't planning to return to the room because she wasn't supposed to. The attorney continued to question if she hated Rick Chance. She said that there were some things about him she didn't like and some things about him she did like. She said he was nice.

The attorney asked Brandi about additional details regarding Robert dumping the contents of the plastic bag the next day. He also referred to the August 15 interview in which she suggested Robert wore another hat on the outside of the mask. The defense attorney also questioned if she intended to have a romantic encounter with Mr. Chance. She said the victim had the presumption that they would have sex and he had touched her intimately just before she left the room. She said that she had asked him to undress when she left the room because she did not want him to follow her out of the room.

Moving to another part of the interview from August 15, the attorney asked about the price tags that were found in the Tempe apartment. In her interview statement about the price tags, she said Robert threw them in the garbage and when asked if she helped, she replied no. But when asked if her fingerprints might be on the price tags, she then responded that she had picked up one of the tags from the floor.

The defense attorney asked Brandi whether she was working in August 2002, and specifically if she was working as an escort. She stated previously that she wasn't working at all. However in her interview, she replied that she was working as an escort. Next, the defense asked Brandi if she had asked her ex-boyfriend Paul to get her a gun, a fake ID and a cell phone account that was not in her own name. She replied that she had asked him for help in getting a gun, but that was at a different time. Previously, she'd had a roommate who was going through a divorce with an abusive spouse and Brandi thought a gun might be needed for protection. Brandi was also asked if she had ever fired a 9 mm Glock and she answered yes.

The defense attorney reviewed the terms of the plea agreement with Brandi. She had pled guilty to second-degree murder, which has a ten-year minimum sentence. On the other hand, first-degree murder has a sentence of natural life or twenty-five years or a death sentence. He pointed out that she had already served three years in county jail and could be eligible to get out in seven years. Finally the defense attorney asked Brandi about the last time she saw Robert. Brandi did not get along with Tara, the mother of Robert's baby, and Brandi said in an interview that she hated Robert and wanted to get on a plane back to Phoenix.

Redirect Examination

The prosecuting attorney referred to the thick binder with transcripts from three interviews. He asked Brandi how many pages were in the transcript from the August 15 interview. She checked through the binder and answered 124 pages. He asked her how many pages were in the second transcript from the August 16th interview. She answered 169 pages. Finally he asked how many pages were included in the transcript of her interview with the defense attorney. It was 76 pages. He pointed out that she had not memorized 370 pages of her interview statements.

The prosecuting attorney also asked Brandi what happened to the business card Rick Chance had given her. She said she threw out his business card. The card she received also had writing on the back of it where Rick Chance wrote the names of jewelers in California. The business card entered in evidence as an exhibit was a different business card. One of the jurors submitted a question about whether the phone number that Brandi received from Robert was the same number that Rick Chance gave her.

One of he jurors submitted a question to the court asking Brandi if she had opened the outside hotel door for Robert. Brandi responded that she did not remember how Robert got into the hotel.

Witness 21: Criminalist Scott Milne, Department of Public Safety

Scott Milne worked in the DNA unit of the DPS Crime Lab and was responsible for testing body fluids. He explained that DNA is a strong exclusionary tool. He had prepared a swab for a DNA profile from the slide of the firearm's action because he'd been advised that the Smith & Wesson pistol had been wiped down and did not have any fingerprints. However, the slide of the firearm had vertical grooves, and so he took a sample from the grooves.

He compared his sample to the DNA profile of three individuals that had been provided to him. The three individuals were Richard Chance, Robert Lemke and Brandi Hungerford. There were multiple peaks on the DNA profile, which indicated that there were multiple contributors to the sample. He was able to exclude both Richard Chance and Brandi Hungerford from the samples of DNA. However, he could not exclude

Robert Lemke's DNA sample as being a match. He stated that in his expert opinion, Robert Lemke was a contributor of DNA to the sample.

Under cross-examination, the defense attorney asked about the three major components of the sample and who the other two contributors were. The criminalist stated that he didn't know who the two others were since he only had a DNA profile of three individuals and two had been excluded.

Exhibit 48

The prosecuting attorney played a recording of a telephone conversation from the Pierce County Jail between Robert and a friend in which Robert conveyed a message for another friend to contact Dan. Robert said he had left a pizza over at Dan's house. In his message, Robert emphasized that Dan needed to get rid of that pizza because it was "going to start smelling real bad." There was a clear sense of urgency, if not panic in Robert's voice as he repeated his instructions to his friend. At the completion of the recorded message, the prosecuting attorney announced that the state rests.

Court recessed for the day at about 4:00 p.m.

Wednesday, September 7, 2005 — 11:00 a.m.

The Defense's Case

Witness 8 (recalled): Detective John Ferrin, Tempe Police Department

The jury viewed a videotape, Exhibit 66. The video showed the third floor area of the hotel in which the murder took place. The video was recorded by the defense. It was stipulated that the video was recent and not recorded at the time of the crime, but no major structural changes had taken place at the hotel. The video began, showing the inside of the elevator doors as they opened and the view moved from the elevator to a semi-circular sitting area. The camera then turned to the left and moved down the corridor. After passing the first inset of two guest room doors, the camera arrived at the second inset of two doors and showed the room number of one of them. This was the entrance to the guest room in which the crime occurred.

Next, the camera was back at the elevators but this time moved right and proceeded up the corridor past the sitting area. Immediately past the sitting area on the left side of the corridor was the entrance to the vending room. The camera then turned back toward the sitting room and far end of the corridor to show the distance from the vending room to the victim's guest room. It was difficult to determine how much Brandi could have seen from the vending room entrance area.

The defense attorney asked the detective to describe the relationship of the elevators to the sitting area, guest room and vending room. The elevator was on the north side of the corridor. The sitting area was opposite the elevators on the south side of the building. The sitting area, guest room and vending room were all on the south side of the corridor with the vending room just west of the elevators and the guest room a relatively short distance down the corridor to the east of the elevators.

11:30 a.m. court recessed for lunch.

The trial was moving right along. Depending on how many witnesses the defense called, we could be getting the case fairly soon. Most of the time when we had a full court day, I would walk a block over to the Phoenix City Hall building and eat in their cafeteria. It was on the eleventh floor and had a nice view of the city, it was quick to get in and out, and best of all, the food was reasonably priced. This had been a popular spot with the men on our jury as well, because of the generous portion sizes. At the lunch break, I decided to just go down to the food courtyard on the ground floor. I purchased a taco lunch and found a table with some of my colleagues.

Ellie came a little later and after lunch we had a brief conversation as we walked back to the security area. She said she had first been leaning one way in the case but later was leaning more the other way. In fact, she said as the case developed her thoughts had gone back and forth more than once, but she wanted to be sure she kept an open mind. She earlier had talked about her children and said she thought about her son and if his fate were up to a jury, she hoped they would give him every benefit of the doubt. I started to feel uncomfortable and made a generalized statement that this would be a difficult decision for everyone and that we would all have to do our best job and vote our conscience based on the facts and instructions we were provided. We were both careful not to say more, but it was clear the pressure was building for everyone on the jury.

1:30 p.m. court reconvened.

Witness 22: Robert Lemke

Robert was born in Boise, Idaho, in November 1977, and grew up in Tacoma, Washington. He had one sister, his mother Peggy, and his father, Robert senior. Robert first visited Arizona in 1998 or 1999 and was living here in August of 2002. He had no family in the Phoenix area. However he had a son who was born on July 3, 2002 from his previous girlfriend Tara, who was living out of state. Under questioning Robert said he had three felony convictions in Washington, as well as one felony conviction in Arizona.

Robert recounted the events of August 8, 2002. Brandi had called him that evening at Mary's apartment. He had a friend named Mims there visiting when he received the call from Brandi. He told Brandi he had company and asked her to call back later. She sounded upset and said she had something important and that she wanted to come over right away. Robert told her that he would be available if she came over in about half an hour. His friend Mims was a Thai woman he had recently met and Robert said he was interested in getting to know her better, possibly even starting a dating relationship with her. Robert had left his car parked down the street at a friend's house. Mims dropped him at his car, and Robert moved his car and returned to Mary's apartment.

Soon thereafter, Brandi knocked at the door. She had her bags with her. She looked as though she had been crying. She had smeared make-up. She took a shower, and afterward, she told Robert she had taken a watch from a client. She said she was worried about the police and asked Robert what she should do. Robert told her she should get rid of whatever she didn't want to have found. He saw a really nice watch in a box and he said he could help her sell it. She also asked him if he could help her sell a gun. They went over to his friend Dan's house that evening to get rid of the gun. After that, he went home to his house in Cave Creek to feed the dogs. His roommate wasn't very good about feeding the dogs and if it were left to her, they might not have water either. Robert and Brandi both slept on Robert's bed that evening in the Cave Creek house.

Robert said he had planned a trip to Tacoma, but he was not planning to take Brandi on the trip because she didn't get along with Tara. On Friday, Robert used Gillian's phone, because his own cell phone didn't work in Tacoma, and he called Mary about returning the Pathfinder to her. He then drove to Mary's apartment. Brandi was driving his Cadillac. They stayed at the apartment briefly and then returned back to the Cave Creek house for dog leashes Robert had forgotten, before starting on their way to Tacoma. When asked about watches Robert said he thought the watch Brandi had might be worth $100,000. Robert said he had three watches: two Rolexes, one of which belonged to a friend, plus a Geneva he'd bought in Hawaii.

Robert's attorney asked about the gun. Robert said he took the gun before he went to his Cave Creek house the first time. He told his friend that it was clean. He had seen the gun before, Brandi had had it and it was Tyler's. Tyler had carried the gun around at different places.

On the trip to Tacoma, Robert drove straight through, only stopping at a few rest areas which he regularly used when he made the trip to Tacoma. His sister lived a short distance from Tacoma and had checked into a hotel. He had intended to stay with his friend Brad for a few days but Brad was out of town for the weekend. Upon reaching Tacoma, Robert first visited his mother at her apartment and then they went to the hotel where his sister was staying. Robert and Brandi stayed at the hotel with his sister until Brad returned. Tara and his son were in Nebraska but he was hoping they would come out for a few days so that he could show off his new son to his family. No one in his family had seen his newborn son yet. He said he was hoping to get back together with Tara.

Robert said he was not aware of the murder and robbery of Rick Chance. When asked how he learned about it, Robert said that they had all gone to dinner at a restaurant and casino, and an old friend of his came by, then left the group and a little later called on Brad's cell phone and asked to talk to Robert. His friend told him, "Your friend is famous. Maybe you should watch the news." Robert then told Brandi, "I think you're on the news." He also advised her, don't talk to your family because they'll know where you're at, meaning the police. He had agreed to help Brandi because he had an expectation of receiving money from the sale of the watch. He told Brandi she shouldn't be walking around if she was on the news. Robert insisted that his only involvement was that he attempted to sell the watch.

The next day, Robert was up early. He was interested in getting a rental car because he didn't want to drive back in Mary's Civic. He was hoping Tara and his son would come back to Arizona with him, and he wanted to drive back with them in a bigger car because he had the two dogs. Brad was driving him to the car rental agency when the police stop occurred. Robert knew he had an outstanding warrant. He said he ran because he was concerned that he would be arrested and he didn't want to go to jail with his son coming. While sitting in the passenger seat, he turned around towards the back seat and told the dogs to stay. His mother was also following Brad and Robert in a rental car. The plan was that she would trade her rental car for the Tahoe and Robert would drive the upgraded vehicle.

After he was arrested, Robert called his friend Matt and told him that his friend Chuey didn't do something he was supposed to. He also wanted to contact Dan about the pizza box. He was concerned about the fact that the gun might be associated with the crime and he didn't want anyone to get in trouble. He had talked to his mother beforehand and she said Brandi had told police that Robert had made her do it. Five juror questions were submitted; two were about his friend Mims and one was about why he didn't ask Brandi more about what was going on.

Cross-Examination

The prosecuting attorney asked Robert about his friend, Mims. Robert said she was a Thai immigrant. He recently met her and had hung out with her a couple of times. He thought she might be someone he would like to get to know better. She had worked at an Asian restaurant in the east valley, but he was unable to locate her after he was arrested. When asked about the gun, Robert said his friend Tyler could document that it was not Robert's gun and that Tyler gave it to Brandi. The attorney also asked Robert why he tried to speak in code when referring to the pizza box. Robert explained he didn't want to get involved and he didn't want to get anyone else in trouble.

The prosecuting attorney asked about the price tags at Mary's apartment. Robert explained that Brandi always carried her luggage with her and he wasn't sure what she might have had in her luggage. The attorney also asked Robert if his friend at the casino could have been a witness for his defense. The attorney asked him why he told Gillian, "If the police call, you haven't seen me." Robert explained that he had a connection with Brandi and if the police contacted Brandi's mother, she would tell the police about Robert. He expected that if the police were in search of Brandi, they might also be in search of him. The attorney also asked about the watches at Brad's loft. Robert said the Chopard watch was not his but that he owned the Geneva watch.

Redirect Examination

Robert's attorney asked him why he was unable to locate Mims or why he couldn't locate Tyler. Robert explained that he had been moved at the county jail a few months ago. After that he did not have possession of any of his own records. After his arrest, he did not have his cell phone records or any other kinds of records available. He also said that many people who might be in a position to help him were not eager to come to court.

In the jury room during an earlier break, Francie had complained to Larry that she could hear loud whispers from the gallery that were very distracting. Larry said he would take care of the problem immediately. Francie sat near the gallery and she was a no-nonsense type of person. I was next to her in line waiting to go through security one day when a man with a briefcase cut in front of everyone. We exchanged glances when it happened and on our way back upstairs we both commented about his lack of common courtesy.

It was now late afternoon, around 3:30 pm, and court recessed for the day. We would return the following afternoon.

Thursday, September 8, 2005 — 1:30 p.m.

Closing Arguments

Prosecution

The prosecuting attorney, Sam Myers, presented his closing arguments with a slide presentation. He went through the chronological order of events and gave an orderly presentation of the evidence. He started with the crime scene and the events surrounding the death of Rick Chance. He summarized the testimony of Brandi Hungerford, who had outlined a plan to drug the victim at his home in order to steal jewelry, and how that plan was modified and ultimately took place at the hotel in Tempe. He outlined the time sequence of the events that occurred the night the victim was killed. First Brandi and Rick Chance had dinner at PF Chang's and then drove to the hotel. Once at the hotel, phone calls were exchanged between Brandi and Robert. Surveillance photos showed Brandi and Rick Chance checking into the hotel. Surveillance photos also showed a male subject on the third floor of the hotel near the vending area and Brandi in the vending area a short time later. The hotel registration information, surveillance cameras and key card all corroborated the timeline of events. Interlaced with this timeline were phone calls placed from or received by Brandi's cell phone. The last call to Brandi's cell phone originated from the coffee shop located next door to the hotel.

The prosecuting attorney continued with a description of the events that occurred after the murder. Brandi and Robert returned to the Tempe apartment, where they cut the tags off of the jewelry. After that they went over to Robert's friend Dan and got rid of the gun that was used in the murder. And finally, they went to Robert's house in Cave Creek where they spent the night. The following morning, they returned briefly to the Tempe apartment and then got on the road and drove straight through to Tacoma. They spent time with Robert's friend Brad and tried to sell some of the jewelry from the robbery. The prosecution reminded the jury of Robert's attempt to avoid capture when he

47

ran at the time of his arrest. And finally, the prosecution replayed an excerpt from the recording of Robert's telephone conversation from jail in which he asked his friend to "get rid of that pizza box because it was going to smell really bad."

At 3:00 p.m. court recessed for the afternoon break
and reconvened about 3:30 p.m.

Defense

The defense attorney, Bruce Peterson, presented his closing arguments using a large white flip chart. He stated that Brandi had lied. She initially said that she told Robert she was on the third floor, but later explained that he had asked her which floor she was on and she replied, "See you in three minutes." She also said when she tried to leave the room she asked the victim to "take off your clothes," which was not consistent with saying to someone on the phone, "see you in three minutes." She had asked her ex-boyfriend to help her obtain a false ID and a gun. The defense pointed out that when the police picked up Brandi in Tacoma, she was alone and not under anyone's control.

Mr. Peterson reminded the jury that it was up to the prosecution to prove beyond a reasonable doubt the guilt of the defendant. He asked the jurors to consider that sometimes events are only a coincidence. He said that a man named Robert Lemke was registered in the hotel at the time of the murder. The police investigation revealed that the Robert Lemke registered at the hotel was a man from Sun City. He stated that there were several areas in which reasonable doubt could not be eliminated. The most critical fact is that no physical evidence from the defendant was found at the crime scene. There were no surveillance photos that could positively identify the defendant, no fingerprints, no DNA except from the gun Robert helped Brandi sell and no eyewitnesses other than Brandi. No one working at either the hotel or the coffee shop identified anyone matching the defendant's description to the police.

Mr. Peterson said he did not know who killed Rick Chance. It could have been Brandi or it could have been someone else such as Brandi's ex-boyfriend. However, it was not the job of the defense to determine who had committed the crime. That was the job of the prosecution. The defense argued that the prosecution failed to prove the defendant had committed the crime. The defense attorney took the classified ad section, Exhibit 45, opened up the pages and reviewed some of the classified ad categories. The prosecution had noted that Rick Chance's ad for Rolex watches was centrally displayed on the folded page. After paging through the section, the defense attorney noted some of the other categories in that classified section were for escort services and guns for sale.

Finally, Mr. Peterson reminded the jury that it had lesser charges to consider. The jury could convict on a charge of theft instead of armed robbery and a charge of conspiracy to commit theft instead of conspiracy to commit armed robbery. The defense counsel readily admitted that his defendant was not a model citizen. The defendant had already testified regarding his willingness to participate in the crime, but only after it had been committed. His involvement was his willingness to help sell a watch that was taken from Rick Chance and to help sell a gun that Brandi had. He said the defendant was guilty of theft, but not the murder and robbery charges. The inconsistencies the defense had pointed out in Brandi's testimony were reason enough to find his client not guilty.

Final Instructions

The judge read ten pages of final jury instructions aloud as the jury followed along with their written copies of the instructions. Then the clerk drew four numbers out of a box and read the names of the four alternates. These jurors would still be on the panel and should be ready to return to serve as a juror if called upon to do so. They were instructed to continue to avoid the news. With twelve women and four men on our panel, I wondered if the ratio of men to women would become any less uneven. Once again random chance took an unexpected turn and three of the four selected as alternates were men. Our jury became eleven women and one man. The one female alternate selected was Debbie, our pregnant juror. At least we would not have to worry about her going into labor in the midst of the deliberations, requiring the jury to start over from the beginning.

At approximately 5:00 p.m. on Thursday afternoon, the trial was over and the jurors at recess, after learning which twelve among the sixteen of them would be deciding the case.

Part 3

The Deliberation

Friday, September 9, 2005

What seemed to be endless days of court and testimony were suddenly over. In between the days in court, we had all doggedly tried to continue with our regular activities as much as possible. Some days we could go to work in the morning and to court in the afternoon. Even though we couldn't watch the local news, we could catch the national news. We were all aware of Hurricane Katrina and the incredible damage it had caused.

By the time closing arguments finished on Thursday afternoon, the entire trial had become somewhat of a blur of one day blending into the next. We had heard from a total of twenty-two witnesses, and some had taken the stand more than once. I hoped my notes would be legible and understandable, now that it was time to rely on them.

Although court never met on Fridays, we could begin our deliberation on Fridays, and so we did. I tried to be sure I was on time on that morning, although I made no effort to arrive early. An earlier arrival only meant that one would stand around outside the security doors waiting for the bailiff to bring the jurors back to the jury room.

The jury room was about fourteen by eighteen feet with a rectangular table in the middle, a square coffee table with some magazines in one corner and a few extra pieces of stored office furniture up against the walls of the room, making it a tight squeeze for one person to move past another. The room had no windows. During the trial, we had each claimed our own unofficially assigned seat in the jury room. I had commandeered a chair in the far corner next to a coat rack. I chose not to sit at the table because there was more legroom in my selected corner. When I entered the jury room for the first day of deliberation, only one empty chair was left—at the corner of the table closest to the door. I quickly grabbed it.

I remembered from my previous experience on a criminal jury the intensity of the deliberation process, and also the solemn intensity of delivering our verdict in court. Our first order of business would be to elect the jury foreperson. Under no circumstances did I want to be that person, but I was confident that out of our group of twelve, someone would be the type to take on the responsibility.

It was amazing to me that a member of our jury also happened to be employed by Superior Court. However, this had its advantages. During the course of the trial, Ginny had helped our bailiff let jurors back through the security doors after breaks. She seemed to be a logical choice for the job of jury foreperson and I was prepared to nominate her if no other volunteers were forthcoming. Everyone had arrived, so we got down to business. Immediately one of the other jurors nominated Ginny as foreperson, she said she would be willing to serve, and we voted her in as our leader. I breathed a small sigh of relief to myself. No way did I want to be the person responsible for ensuring that the jury followed its instructions, nor did I want to be the person who signed the verdict, particularly if we found this defendant guilty.

We began to review our notes and list the evidence. According to our instructions, the evidence was both the testimony of the witnesses and the exhibits introduced in court. We had an easel with flip-chart paper, and Ginny started writing down the different exhibits. We went through our notes as a group and wrote down the different items as they appeared in our notes.

A cardboard box sitting on a metal cabinet in the corner of the room contained all the exhibits. Various items associated with the crime were in plastic bags; we received a box of disposable gloves to use when handling those items. We had Exhibit 43, the registration record, and Exhibit 41, a printout of the room status from the hotel. We had several photos from the surveillance video: Exhibit 52, the photo of the front desk that showed Brandi and Rick Chance at check-in; Exhibit 53, a photo of the circular drive and Brandi and Rick Chance walking towards the parking lot; Exhibit 51, a female subject in the vending machine room on the third floor; and Exhibit 50, a male subject in the hallway walking past the entrance to the third floor vending room.

Exhibit 56 was a diagram showing the location of the victim's gunshot wound. Exhibit 54 was a diagram of the crime scene. It showed the location of the furniture in the room and the location and position of the victim lying on the floor. There were also photos of the bedspread showing bloodstains on the corner and on the far side of the spread. There were two pictures of the victim: one taken from the entrance to the room, and one showing the pool of blood on the floor where the victim had been lying. We also had exhibits of the jewelry tags and the torn up note found in the trash in front of the Cave Creek house.

The Toyota 4Runner had a business card for Empire Glass stuffed between the seat and the console. It was Exhibit 36. Exhibit 46 was the black gym bag Brad delivered to the Tacoma Police Department. Other exhibits from the Phoenix area included Exhibit 44, a copy of the receipt for the Chopard watch. Exhibit 58 was a photo of the Chopard watch. It had a large square face with a square inset pattern of diamonds, and framed with more diamonds around the face, plus rows of diamonds inset in the links of the watchband. Exhibit 45 was the classified ad section, and Exhibit 17 was a photograph showing the location of the classified ads tucked between the driver's seat and the console of Robert's Cadillac.

Exhibit 27 was the Smith & Wesson 9 mm pistol, including the magazine and one loose round. Only the recovered handgun, not the magazine or the round, was admitted into evidence as Exhibit 27.001. The Judge did not want to provide the jury with an exhibit that was in effect a loaded gun. Exhibit 48 was a cassette tape recording of the defendant's jail conversation, telling his friend about the pizza box.

The defense had entered only one exhibit into evidence: Exhibit 66 was a video the defense had filmed of the area outside the crime scene, including an elevator, the sitting area across from the elevators, the vending room location, and the location of the guest room door on the third floor of the hotel. The video was entered into evidence with the stipulation that it was recent and had only been filmed a few months ago, rather than at the time of the crime.

Our notes seemed consistent with one another, which was encouraging. By lunch we had identified and listed all the exhibits in our notes, as well as our inventory of the box of evidence that had been placed in the jury room. We discovered that not all the exhibits referred to during the trial had been admitted as evidence. The attorneys had referred to transcripts of interviews when they asked key witnesses, particularly Brandi, about various events, but the jury did not receive a copy of the transcripts. If we had received copies of all of those transcripts, the jury might still be reviewing the evidence.

We took a break for lunch and when we returned, began to review which pieces of evidence were the most credible. We paged through our notes in sequence of testimony. We started with the timeline based on the hotel records, telephone records and photos from the surveillance tapes.

The detective who had checked out the surveillance system testified that the time stamp on the tapes was about twenty minutes fast, so we subtracted twenty minutes from the time stamp in each of the video surveillance photos. The photo at the registration desk was 9:34 p.m., so we adjusted the time to 9:14 p.m. The credit card receipt was run at 9:16 p.m. The key card for the hotel guest room was used once around 9:19 p.m. Brandi placed a call from her cell phone to the Tempe apartment at 9:08 p.m. and the call from the coffee shop to Brandi's cell phone was placed at 9:28 p.m. The first photo from the third floor vending machine was the unidentified male subject. It was date stamped at 9:55 p.m., which we adjusted to 9:35 p.m. The second photo from the third-floor vending machine showed a female subject, Brandi. It was stamped at 10:03 p.m., so we adjusted the time to 9:43 p.m.

After we finished our list of exhibits, we started reviewing each witness in the order they testified. This process did not go smoothly. We spent the remainder of the afternoon engaging in spontaneous discussions over various pieces of the testimony and exhibits. Ours was a group of people who had a lot on their minds and had been waiting for quite some time to express thoughts about all they had learned over the past weeks. Some thought the evidence was obvious and convincing while others thought the evidence required closer examination.

We were all feeling the intensity and enormity of the task. We sporadically abandoned any semblance of an orderly process in which everyone took turns sharing comments. At times there were two or three debates going on in various corners of the room, and the competing conversations were not allowing everyone to hear all of the comments being offered. I felt compelled to say something, so I said I was having trouble listening to all the comments from around the room and asked that only one person speak at a time. The process became more orderly. We were not angry or shouting, but often times one another's comments were interrupted by someone else's pent-up urge to speak up. The weeks spent sitting in silence and just listening had taken their toll.

By the time we took our afternoon break, everyone was in need of a time-out. Ginny and I both sat at the end of the table closest to the door, so we were among the first out of the room. We rounded the corner and as Ginny passed through the security doors in front of me, I heard her say to no one in particular, "Well, I guess this is going to take a little longer than I thought." We returned from our break and continued to make limited progress with our discussion for the remainder of the afternoon.

By the end of the day, most of the jurors opted to walk the two blocks to the parking garage instead of waiting for the jury shuttle bus. The weather had eased up from the August heatwave and we welcomed the opportunity to stretch our legs. Ginny and Ellie were one or two strides ahead of Abby and me. I thought I heard Ellie ask Ginny a question about her job with the court. Ginny responded that she thought she could be an impartial juror because even if she happened to know about the defendant's prior convictions, she would not let that information influence her and would not share such information with other jurors. I couldn't really hear what the conversation was about, but the subject was dropped and I was glad that the conversation ended apparently as quickly as it began.

Monday, September 12, 2005

The weekend passed quickly, and everyone returned on Monday morning feeling a bit more rested and more prepared to tackle the job before us. We continued to discuss some of the exhibits and testimony of the case. Sometimes we found ourselves speculating over details we had not received. We kept returning to the events at the murder scene and discussing what things we did know and what things we did not know. Had there been a struggle? Did the victim see his assailant enter the room, or did his assailant surprise him? Where were the two standing when the shot was fired? How quickly did the chain of events take place?

When we first started deliberations, our bailiff had cautioned us not to reinvent the wheel. I wondered if that was what we were doing. We only had a certain amount of information, and there was no way to augment the information regardless of how helpful we thought it would be. Everyone was in a calmer frame of mind and our discussions continued in a more orderly fashion.

At the lunch break, several of us went to the fast food area outside the first floor of the courthouse. This was near the front entrance to the building, and frequently the location where the local TV channels would set up a remote broadcast site. A group of us found a table outside and sat together. Two of us had noticed some people associated with our case were in the lunch area, which puzzled us somewhat since we were in the midst of our deliberation. We also noticed one of the local news channels had its truck parked across the street with the boom up as though they were prepared to broadcast some sort of courthouse update. Something was going on, but there were plenty of other trials in progress besides ours. We finished our lunch, stretched our legs and returned to the jury room.

Once everyone was back in the jury room, Larry came and asked us to take a break from our deliberations. That seemed odd. He wanted us to just stop deliberating for about twenty minutes. He had been working with various jurors, helping them complete paperwork for reimbursement under the state's lengthy trial program. Larry took this opportunity to call one or two jurors out of the room in order to assist with their paperwork. First Ellie left to work on her forms, and once she returned Larry called out Ivy. When they both had returned, Larry asked Ginny if she would step out for a moment. That seemed odd because Ginny was a court employee and would receive her regular pay. After about ten or fifteen minutes, Larry came back again and asked where Ginny's personal belongings were. We found her purse and lunch bag and passed them over to Larry. He thanked us and left the room. Shortly after that, he returned to let us know that Ginny had been excused as a juror and that we would be hearing more about this from the judge.

After the usual twenty minutes of waiting around for the court to assemble, the eleven remaining jurors filed into a nearly empty courtroom. Judge Rayes explained that the attorneys opted not to be present, but that one of our jurors had been excused. The judge reminded us of the admonitions that we should not talk about the case with one another unless we were all together in the jury room. That meant not during breaks and not on the way to or from the parking garage. He said no one had done anything wrong, but just wanted to remind us of our instructions. He also explained that now that a juror had been excused, the court would bring back one of the alternates and the jury must stop deliberating at this time. A name had been drawn from the alternates and Debbie would rejoin us tomorrow morning.

The fickle finger of probability had struck again. How were the three male alternates beaten out by the odds? Debbie would be a good juror, but I wondered if her baby would wait to be born until after the trial. If not, the jury would have to begin all over for a third time with its deliberation process. Ginny's departure also meant we would have to elect a new foreperson. This had been a very eventful day.

Tuesday, September 13, 2005

Tuesday morning arrived, and our newly defined panel of twelve filed back into the courtroom to receive our instructions again from the judge. We returned to the jury room with only minor alterations in our self-assigned seats as Debbie assumed her regular chair at the far end of the table from the door. I was still sitting at the end of the table next to the door. Larry came and told us we should start with the selection of our foreperson and then review all the evidence again, starting from the beginning.

I was going to suggest we begin by checking to see if anyone wanted to volunteer to be the foreperson, but Ellie spoke up right away and asked if I would be the foreperson because she thought I would listen to others. One or two others quickly joined the bandwagon. Momentum was growing for my impending appointment. I suspected my plea for a more orderly deliberation the previous Friday was coming back to haunt me, lamely asked if anyone else would volunteer, and, of course, got no response. I was forming my own opinion about the case just like everyone else, but it seemed important to select someone who was considered neutral by the other jurors. I agreed to be the foreperson and we were off on our second start. In order to save some time, we agreed to break early for about twenty minutes and bring back our lunch to the jury room.

We welcomed Debbie and were happy to have her join us. She asked what had happened and we told her that we weren't given any information about why Ginny was excused. Debbie said she had enjoyed her weekend because she had four days of being totally away from the trial, never having a glimmer of an idea that she would be asked to return on Tuesday. She was a little concerned that the rest of us might be impatient while she was brought up to speed. Debbie was just finishing her master's degree in English and took very good notes. Everyone agreed that a second review of our notes along with hers would be helpful in finding additional detail or clarification of the information previously reviewed. Betty sat at the corner of the table next to the flip chart and volunteered to write down a summary of our notes on the chart.

We made steady progress throughout the afternoon, no doubt because we were now experienced at this particular activity. When we returned from afternoon break, Christie, one of our younger jurors, mentioned that she had run into Ginny the previous afternoon when she was waiting for her ride. They had just said hello and asked how each other was doing. Christie explained that she shared one car in her family and often had to wait for someone to pick her up after court. Ellie spoke up and said she lived in the same part of town as Christie and would give her a ride. Christie usually worked two jobs and jury duty was a big challenge. Ellie, a parent with a son about the same age as Christie, insisted that the two carpool together and announced that she would pick her up starting immediately.

At the end of the day, I asked each person to share their thoughts about the information we had, its strengths, and what additional information would be needed to help the group reach a decision. We were working together cooperatively as a jury but I needed to be sure we received some input from everyone. Tuesday was a productive day.

On the days when court was scheduled for morning and afternoon, I did not go to my office first, but directly to court. I wanted to have a clear head and knew if I went to work, I would get caught up with the day's challenges and be either distracted or late or both when I arrived in court. By now my ongoing concentration on the trial was clearly having an impact. I was waking up at two or three a.m., without being able to get back to sleep on a fairly regular basis.

The next morning, the incident about the two jurors carpooling was on my mind. Although I thought it was a nice gesture, we had received no shortage of admonitions about contact with one another as well as those in court. I decided that I should make the court aware of what was happening. I found Larry's business card and called his office, hoping I wouldn't have to leave a message. I was in luck — he answered his phone. I explained that Christie had seen Ginny after Ginny was excused, but they had just exchanged pleasantries and now Ellie had volunteered to give Christie a ride every day. He thanked me for the information and said I should continue to report anything I thought was important. Larry was a master at giving positive feedback while remaining neutral about the information provided. I didn't know if this was a problem or not, but at least now the court could decide how to handle the situation.

Wednesday, September 14, 2005

On Wednesday we went as a group through our notes one last time and identified all of the facts presented, but this time without passing judgment on their relevance, importance or credibility. We had very strong agreement on the collective contents of our notes, so it appeared we had all heard essentially the same information. At the end of the day, I asked each juror to give a summary of his or her views on the credibility of the evidence. In the midst of our individual summaries, Larry entered the room and asked how we were doing. We had not given him much information on our progress. He said he would order pizza for us on Friday if we were still deliberating, and I replied that we should be taking a vote fairly soon.

Everyone agreed that the timeline information was most important to the case. Everyone agreed that the evidence presented by the police and by individuals not directly involved in the crime seemed very credible. And everyone agreed that the information given by Brandi and Robert seemed the least credible since both would have reason to lie about what actually happened.

Debbie commented that our next step would be to determine the credibility of Brandi and Robert's testimonies, based on the corroboration of the other evidence. We ended the day by reading over all of the jury instructions together as a group. Wednesday was another very productive day.

Thursday, September 15, 2005

It looked like Thursday would be our day of decision. We had a strong foundation based on a thorough review of the evidence and testimony. We had viewed all of the exhibits one or more times over the past two days. We'd discussed our theories about the murder based on the diagram of the crime scene and the diagram of the victim and his wounds. We'd passed the murder weapon around the table without removing it from its plastic bag. We had reviewed the hotel records and our notes of the timeline for cell phone calls. We had become familiar with all of the items in the evidence box. It was down to the testimony of Brandi versus Robert.

Some jurors thought Robert was more convincing and had a much more personable manner than Brandi, yet no one thought Robert's explanation of the events was at all credible. He talked about getting to know Mims as a possible romantic interest, and later said that when he went to Tacoma, he was hopeful that he and Tara could get back together. Robert's explanation of the call from Brandi made no sense, because the phone and hotel records indicated that her call was placed before the crime took place. He also seemed to drop everything he was doing to devote all of his efforts to helping Brandi after she called him. He said the reason for the pizza box phone call was because he didn't want to get anyone in trouble, and yet in that same taped conversation he referred to Brandi as a bitch that set him up.

Some jurors thought Brandi was not convincing, and that she had a cold, impersonal manner—yet everyone agreed that her version of the events corroborated with the timeline. To those jurors who questioned her credibility, Brandi seemed to be defensive or at times uncooperative toward the defense attorney's questions. There had been several exchanges in which Mr. Peterson had asked about comments from the transcripts of her previous interviews, and she would only respond by stating, "That's what it says."

During Brandi's testimony she and the defense attorney had been engaged in a contest to see if the attorney could catch Brandi in a statement that would contradict any previous statement from the hundreds of pages of recorded interviews. Brandi had been slow, deliberate and occasionally unresponsive as she answered questions about her earlier interviews.

After debating the credibility of the two key witnesses throughout the morning, we re-read the instructions on proof beyond a reasonable doubt and stopped for our lunch break. When we returned from lunch, we agreed to take our first vote. We started with Count Three, Conspiracy to Commit Armed Robbery. We decided to go with a secret ballot and distributed slips of paper. After a few minutes, we collected everyone's vote. Holly was sitting to my left and I asked her to look on as I read each vote aloud and Betty marked down the results: eleven Guilty and one Not Guilty. We discussed whether or not we were comfortable as a group in revealing our individual votes since we couldn't effectively discuss the objections of the person who voted not guilty without knowing what their objections were.

Ivy spoke up almost immediately and said she thought everyone knew she was the 'not guilty' vote and she didn't have any problem discussing it openly. To her, everything was either black or white. She had been surprised when the prosecution rested its case because she was still waiting for some kind of information that explicitly demonstrated guilt.

Ellie also spoke up, saying she had a difficult time making her decision and felt a little pressured while we were conducting the ballot because she really needed additional time to think about which way to vote.

Our opinions were now out in the open and not unanimous. We were all feeling the pressure of our obligation but there was an atmosphere of respect for each person's opinion. We proceeded to vote on the other counts with just a show of hands. We voted nine Guilty and three Not Guilty for Count Two, Armed Robbery. We tackled the remaining Count One, First Degree Murder, and voted eight Guilty and four Not Guilty.

Once again, we went around the room, this time asking each juror to explain their vote. We easily identified the key points for the not guilty votes. Our instructions for murder stated that the crime requires proof that the defendant committed armed robbery. Our instructions for armed robbery stated that the crime requires proof that the defendant committed a robbery. Those who voted not guilty pointed to the lack of physical proof that the defendant was ever at the crime scene. Without Brandi's testimony, we could not place him at the scene.

It was time to report our progress. The front corner of the room had a small counter and coffee area and against the back wall was a small button that set off a buzzer in the bailiff's office. We pushed the button and waited. Larry entered the room and we told him the outcome of our vote. He explained that I needed to complete one of the forms for submitting questions to the judge and write that the jury had reached an impasse. He also asked me to complete the verdict forms. There were five forms, one for each of the three counts and one for each of the two lesser counts. I quickly filled out the questionnaire, stating the jury had reached an impasse, and returned it to Larry. He left the room with our note to the judge and I reviewed the verdict forms with the other jurors.

All of the verdict forms had a check box for Guilty or Not Guilty. The forms for both the robbery and theft charges also had check boxes for the value of the stolen property. The three forms for the original count would only need my signature; neither of the two boxes for Guilty/Not Guilty should be checked. For the two lesser counts of theft and conspiracy to commit theft, we still needed to vote. I read over the information on the conspiracy to commit theft charge and asked for a show of hands. Twelve jurors raised their hands—the defendant was guilty. We repeated the procedure for the theft charge with the same result. We had a verdict. It was late in the afternoon and I buzzed Larry again to let him know we were ready to go home for the day.

It sounded as though Larry would have to do some serious juggling with the Friday court calendar. He explained that we would have to be in court in the morning so the judge could explain the impasse instructions to us. We put all of our notebooks in a cabinet as was our usual routine and I placed the verdict forms in the cabinet as well. Everyone filed out with a sense of relief. We had reached a verdict on the lesser counts, and soon this burden would be lifted.

My office was only a few minutes' drive from the court building and even if it was near quitting time I usually stopped by after court each day to catch up on my email, check on project deadlines, answer any stray questions, etc. When I arrived, one of the managers made a point to ask me how I was doing. A couple of nearby coworkers waited for my reaction. With dramatic emphasis I said, "Fine, thank you very much," and got a laugh. It seemed that my staff always knew about the latest development in court by the time I arrived at the office and I was sure they had already heard that the jury was deadlocked. I had not told anyone what trial I was assigned to, but everyone knew from my schedule it was the Rick Chance murder trial.

Friday, September 16, 2005

Friday morning I arrived at court feeling as though this would undoubtedly be the final day of my jury duty. This had been an intense experience and my work responsibilities had not gone away during the trial. My catch-phrase at work was that jury duty is not a walk in the park. Everyone arrived in the jury room. Holly said she had a question she still wanted to ask about, so we told Larry we would need a few minutes before we were ready to go into court. We joked with him and said we had held out until Friday so we could get our pizza. Larry left the room and we got down to business. Holly said she wondered why Robert was arrested first. Both went to Tacoma together, yet Robert was arrested immediately and Brandi wasn't arrested even after her first interview with police. We debated that briefly.

Two jurors said they'd had second thoughts after leaving court Thursday evening and would change their vote from Guilty to Not Guilty if we had to vote all over again on the major counts. We had a more relaxed discussion of the key factors in the case, and took another vote just to be sure. The vote was exactly the same. Nevertheless, it was helpful to spend some time revisiting our discussion from Thursday. We were moving toward closure. We realized that Larry hadn't returned after a few minutes, so we buzzed his office and let him know we were ready to go into court. While we waited, Ivy said she wanted to tell me what had happened earlier when Ginny was excused. She wanted me to know since I was the one who ended up taking over as foreperson. I said it wasn't important and that we probably shouldn't share information until after we were all excused. Francie told us that the whispers she'd heard earlier were from the victim's family saying "liar" during the defendant's testimony. Larry arrived and told us it would be about twenty minutes before we could begin, so we could take a quick break.

We returned to the jury room from break and lined up in order to file into the courtroom. We took our seats and Judge Rayes thanked us for all of our efforts but asked us to try again to reach a decision. We received a copy of the impasse instructions and the judge read them aloud to us. We filed back into the jury room.

It was time to order that pizza. Larry must have connections with every pizza and deli within the area. Everybody went in different directions to get a beverage or a smoke or just a walk in the fresh air. We all returned from our destinations, the pizza arrived and we were back at work. We had debated the case several times. Ellie suggested that it would make more sense for the majority to make their best case to influence the minority to change their mind.

The majority position was based on logic and deductive reasoning. Our instructions stated that evidence may be direct or circumstantial. Circumstantial evidence is the proof of a fact from another fact. The first fact was that Rick Chance was killed and robbed. The second fact was that Brandi was involved in the crime. Her involvement had to be based on one of three possible scenarios. First, she acted alone, second, she acted with someone else or third, she acted with Robert. It did not seem reasonable that she acted alone. If she had acted alone, she could have picked a more private location in which she was not filmed by surveillance cameras several times. It was unlikely that a petite woman acting alone would pistol-whip a large man. If she had acted with someone else, there would be an association with that person. The first two scenarios were also inconsistent with the rest of the evidence, particularly the sequence of phone calls and her association with Robert and the stolen articles.

Based on cell phone and hotel records, Brandi's first call to Robert occurred before the crime was committed. Yet Robert testified that Brandi had already taken the watch from her client and was upset when she called him. Robert made immediate and extensive use of his contacts after the crime. He got rid of the gun immediately and left town the very next day. He took Brandi to Tacoma with him, even though he and several of his friends stated that Brandi didn't get along with Tara, the person he said he planned to see. Tara lived in Nebraska and apparently never showed up in Washington. Robert said the pistol was Brandi's but it excluded her DNA. During the high-risk felony stop, Robert ran from police who had weapons drawn. Every person associated with the murder weapon cooperated with the police in its recovery, except Robert. If Robert had not been involved in the crime, he should have been the first to help the police recover the murder weapon. The only possible scenario was that Brandi acted with Robert.

After the review of the guilty scenario, we agreed that the majority should also hear from the minority. In fact, several of those who had voted guilty said they would welcome information that would allow them to change their vote. No one wanted to rush to a guilty verdict.

The minority position was based on lack of convincing evidence. There was no physical evidence connecting Robert to the crime scene. Brandi's testimony was the only available evidence for a guilty verdict. Ellie said she knew of someone who had agreed to a plea bargain and consequently lied to implicate someone else in another crime. She would question anyone whose testimony was based on a plea bargain. Those who voted not guilty agreed that Robert probably was a participant in the crime, but even for the count on conspiracy to commit armed robbery, there was no proof that Robert was aware of any plan to use a gun.

We had given the deliberation another effort, yet again. We took another vote:

Count Three, Conspiracy to Commit Armed Robbery:
nine guilty, three not guilty

Count Two, Armed Robbery: nine guilty, three not guilty

Count One, First Degree Murder: eight guilty, four not guilty.

We were finished. We felt helpless, but there was nothing left for us to do. We desperately wanted to do our job. We looked over the impasse instructions. They stated that we could identify the areas of agreement and disagreement. We decided it would be due diligence to communicate this information to the court, so we sent a note out to the judge that we had one key issue on which we disagreed—the presence of the defendant at the crime scene.

We knew the court was not in a position to help and it was no surprise when we received a response back that essentially restated a portion of the jury instructions. We must determine the facts from the evidence presented in court through testimony and exhibits.

We again looked over the impasse instructions. They stated that we could tell the attorneys and the judge which issues we needed assistance with. We came up with four questions that some jurors really wanted to know more about, but we knew in advance the answers would not be forthcoming. We discussed how we wanted to ask the questions and I wrote them down on four separate forms:

Were all phone calls placed by Brandi and Robert from the Tacoma jail reviewed by the police?
Can we see the hotel pictures without enlargement or enhancement?
Why was the defendant pursued as a suspect so quickly?
Was Brandi's ex-boyfriend an investigative lead?

Not long after we submitted our questions, Larry returned the forms with our answers, now numbered two through five. The answer to question two was exactly what we expected: "We must determine the facts from the evidence admitted at trial. No new evidence will be submitted". The answer to the third question was that the photos were not enhanced. We should have used the word pixilated because we didn't mean to suggest that the photos had been changed. The answer to questions four and five was "See answer to #2." We enjoyed a little comic relief as I read those two responses back to the rest of the jury.

That was it. We went around to everyone once again and unanimously voted guilty on the lesser charges of theft. I completed the verdict forms and we buzzed for Larry. He came to the jury room, we told him our outcome and also completed another jury question form, stating that we disagreed on one key issue, the presence of the defendant at the hotel/crime scene. Larry took the jury form and explained that we would go back into court to deliver the verdict.

I wondered if we would be released from jury duty afterward. The trial had taken its toll on all of us and everyone knew it was about to end. Everyone had talked about losing sleep and lately some jurors had no appetite for food. We knew the media had reported on this case and a camera was in the courtroom most of the time. The media could not approach us as long as we were impaneled and we were all careful about wearing our juror badges during breaks throughout the trial. We had discussed the prospect of being interviewed right after the trial and we were unanimous in that everyone felt like an emotional wreck and no one wanted to talk to the media. We asked Larry about the media and he explained that once we were released as jurors, it would probably be up to us whether we wanted to talk to reporters. He also said we could expect to hear from reporters after the trial because our names were public record, unless we requested to have the records sealed. Larry also said the attorneys might want to talk to us about the trial and we were all fine with that idea.

It was time to file into court. This time, there was a tremendous feeling of tension as we lined up in our accustomed order. I carried the file folder with the completed verdict forms. We took our places and I looked around the room. In addition to the usual deputy assigned to the defense table, there were four deputies standing in a solid line blocking the entrance doors to the courtroom. The Sheriff's Department had obviously taken note of the defendant's prior effort to run from police. The judge asked if we had a verdict. I don't recall what happened next, but I think I said yes and handed the folder to Larry as he approached the jury box. The clerk read the verdicts aloud and I was thankful that she said "signed by the jury foreperson" rather than reading my name.

It was over. We were done. I looked forward to having a marathon conversation over the weekend to start getting the experience behind me. Unbelievably, Judge Rayes thanked the jury and asked us to return on Monday. Because we had found the defendant guilty of the lesser charges, we must return to consider aggravation. Court adjourned and we all returned to the jury room in a daze.

Jackie was sobbing and going through tissues non-stop. Larry explained that jurors often feel a sense of frustration or failure if they cannot reach a verdict but told us we had all done a good job. He also reminded us that the court offers counseling for jurors who have suffered stress or trauma from their service. Jackie assured us she was fine but others expressed apprehension about leaving the building. Since we were still impaneled, the media could not talk to us. Yet several jurors were very nervous about leaving, now that the verdict was out. Larry arranged for a Sheriff's deputy to take us down the service elevator and escort us to the side entrance. We walked down the hallway and all piled into the elevator with our escort. When we reached the ground floor, everything was normal, except for us, and we filtered out of the building as usual. I returned to my office and as I encountered coworkers, I stopped them in mid-sentence to let them know I still wasn't at liberty to talk. It would be a long weekend.

Monday, September 19, 2005

On Monday morning I prepared to go into court, and wondered how long it might take to go through this next phase. I arrived at court, passed through security, and reported to the jury room. It was once again crowded with jurors and alternates. Our three remaining alternates were undoubtedly the most uninformed people in town. They had been instructed to continue to avoid the news and did not know we had reached a verdict. We told them the outcome but there was no time to answer the many questions that would have followed.

Larry came in and explained that we would not have to complete the aggravation phase, and that we were all finished with our job as jurors. He welcomed the three alternate men and joked that our single male juror was no doubt glad to see them. Larry quipped that Mike had taken up knitting after spending so much time with the women. We also advised the men that the eleven women had virtually taken over both restrooms in the jury room during the course of the trial. We were ready to line up by number and enter court. There was a little extra maneuvering this morning, as we tried to regroup with our three alternates in numerical order.

We entered the courtroom, took our seats and Judge Rayes began his remarks. He welcomed one and all and thanked us for the job we had done. He explained that it would not be necessary for the jury to deal with the next phase of the trial. The judge could determine sentencing based on the prior convictions of the defendant. He then explained that on occasion it just turns out that the jury cannot reach a decision, as it did for our jury. He assured us this is part of the process as well and that we shouldn't have any thoughts or feelings that we did less than our duty. He explained that it had been a difficult case and we had done the best job that we could. He knew it had been a hardship for all of us to break away from our regular lives over the last several weeks and said we would no longer be under any of the admonitions. We could watch the news, talk about the case to anyone, and resume our lives.

He then offered to help us catch up on the news by informing us that there had been a hurricane named Katrina and the Cardinals had lost their first two games. We all laughed with both anxiety and relief. Judge Rayes thanked us once again, excused us and we filed back into the jury room.

Inside the jury room, Larry asked if we wanted to talk to the attorneys. We did. He also asked if Rick Chance's personal attorney could join us. We were fine with that. Larry said we could ask the attorneys any questions we wanted, but they could not ask us questions. The alternates could also remain if they wanted. As we waited for the attorneys, Ivy took the opportunity to explain that Ginny had made comments about the case to Ellie and to her, and they had notified the bailiff. I had assumed this was more or less what happened, but I appreciated her sharing the information with me.

Soon the room was filled with three people from the prosecuting attorney's office, the Tempe case management detective, two defense attorneys and Rick Chance's attorney. Our fourteen by eighteen-foot jury room was bursting with about two dozen people. It was almost like going backstage after a performance. We started to ask questions and so did the attorneys. We tried to provide general statements without answering the direct questions, but then Larry checked with Judge Rayes and returned to inform us that questions from attorneys were okay.

The two opposing attorneys stood next to each other, looking totally relaxed and at ease. They had been very formal and polite to one another throughout the trial and we had noted that they didn't engage in any of the dramatic behavior we'd all watched on television dramas. Now they spoke freely and smiled or laughed at some of our jabs. We told the prosecuting attorneys that we might have been able to find the defendant guilty of the conspiracy charge, had we known more regrding the chain of possession of the gun.

At least two witnesses referred to Tyler, but we never heard from him regarding whether or not Brandi received the gun. Someone asked the question about why the defendant was arrested so quickly and why it took longer to arrest Brandi. We thought it would have been helpful to have specific information on whether the ex-boyfriend had been checked out as a lead. The prosecuting attorneys took lots of notes. Mr. Peterson asked what we thought about the defendant's credibility as a witness. We told him Robert had the least credibility of any witness and although he seemed at ease and even affable in front of the jury, we rated him with nearly zero credibility. Rick Chance's attorney stood quietly and seemed content just to listen to the exchange among the jurors and the trial attorneys.

The debriefing was over after about ten or fifteen minutes. We were free to go and everyone was in a much more stable state of mind to run the gauntlet of any reporters that might be waiting for us downstairs. Larry encouraged everyone to take their notebooks with them. Based on prior jury experience, I had assumed we would leave our notebooks behind, but decided to take mine with me.

When I reached the ground floor, I was walking alongside Abby, one of the first jurors I'd met. We encountered a reporter just before reaching the west entrance to the building. He asked us if he could interview us and we said we'd rather not. Then he asked if we knew that the defendant was also accused of committing a similar robbery with Gillian as his accomplice. Abby replied that we did not know. The reporter continued and asked if that information would have influenced our decision. Abby said it would not have been relevant to our case and I responded that I did not wish to be interviewed.

We reached the west entrance, the jury bus was parked at the curb, and we climbed on board. Within just a few minutes we were headed for the parking garage.

I walked to my car and got in. I did not return to my office to check my email. Instead, I called my sister and drove directly over to her house where I proceeded to bend her ear with a marathon account of my experience. She listened attentively and let me just unload until I ran out of things to say.

By the time I finished talking, it was time for the local news. I happened to be looking toward the television and saw my fellow juror, Mike, being interviewed. As the only male juror, he was being asked if he thought the outcome might have been different if there were other men on the jury. He tried to speculate as best he could, but I could see the tension in his face. We were all going to be recovering jurors for a while, and I was grateful that Mike had taken the time to stop and talk to reporters. The media had gotten the juror perspective and the rest of us were off the hook. Now it was time for all of us to return to our normal lives.

Epilogue

During the height of the deliberations, it was difficult not reaching a verdict. It was frustrating, but I truly thought that each person on the jury had done the best job they could of considering the evidence and making a decision. I have nothing but respect for everyone who served on that trial.

I still have lingering questions and most of them can never be answered. We will never know exactly what happened in the hotel room where Rick Chance lost his life. The jury vote was eight to four for murder and nine to three for armed robbery. Our youngest juror voted 'guilty' on armed robbery and 'not guilty' on murder. Three jurors were not going to change their 'not guilty' vote on both charges, so the logic behind the split vote of a fourth juror was never asked for or offered. As for the impasse, I have equal respect for the nine who voted 'guilty' and the three or four who voted 'not guilty'. Both sides had a reasoned and sincere point of view. We were given a definition of reasonable doubt, but each of the jurors had to apply that definition as best they could. I believe each juror voted his or her conscience.

Robert Lemke received a sentence of twenty-seven years for his conviction of theft and conspiracy to commit theft. I am content with the outcome. The case was not retried, because in September 2007 Lemke pleaded guilty to first degree murder and confessed to shooting Rick Chance. In return, he received a life sentence with possibility of parole after twenty-five years. In October 2007, Brandi Hungerford was sentenced to fourteen years in prison. I hope this sentencing, and especially Lemke's confession, will bring closure to Rick Chance's family and friends.

The overall process worked, and our role was only one part of the larger process. At the beginning of the trial when I had to search out my emotions and moral position on the death penalty, I was troubled by the fact that our defendant might receive the death sentence for a single murder while a convicted murderer known as BTK could perform several brutal murders and receive a life sentence in another state. The fact that one state has the death penalty and another state doesn't, will long be the subject of debate. Yet

I resolved that in a civilized society you must be willing to carry out the rule of law. We are also blessed to live in a society where anyone can work to change the rule of law through our legislative process if one feels the need to do so.

On a grander scale, I know it was a great honor to have this chance to participate in one of the most important institutions of our democracy. The news reminds us every day that not all countries have the right to a trial by jury. Our process may not be perfect, but I am convinced more than ever that it works better than any other process. I also have a deep sense of respect for the attorneys, as both represented their side very well. I am particularly grateful to know that there are people willing to work so hard to defend those accused of a crime. This defendant received a strong defense, not a token effort.

As I was writing up my notes, it seemed especially tragic to learn that in Saddam Hussein's trial in Iraq, some defense attorneys were assassinated. I'm sure this experience has forever changed my twelve colleagues and me. I am extremely grateful for the experience, now that it is over.

Nevertheless—after the trial I did ask Larry if the court could provide me with a lifetime get-out-of-jury-duty card.

SUPERIOR COURT OF ARIZONA
IN MARICOPA COUNTY
Central Court Building, 201 W. Jefferson Suite 11C

From the Chambers of
Hon. Douglas L. Rayes

Phoenix AZ 85003
602-506-0816

APPENDIX:

Juror Oaths: Screening Panel

Juror Questionnaire

Juror Oaths: Final Jury

List of Jurors

Preliminary Jury Instructions

Trial Days

Questions by Jurors

Final Jury Instructions

Impasse Instructions

List of Witnesses

List of Exhibits Provided to Jury

Images of Key Exhibits

Photo of Defendant at Time of Arrest

Appendix 1

JUROR OATHS

SCREENING PANEL

You (and each of you) do solemnly swear that you will true answers make to all questions asked by the Court and counsel touching upon your qualifications to serve as a trial juror in the case now on trial, so help you God?

Appendix 2

JUROR QUESTIONNAIRE
INSTRUCTIONS

IN THE SUPERIOR COURT OF THE STATE OF ARIZONA
IN AND FOR THE COUNTY OF MARICOPA

STATE OF ARIZONA,	No. CR2002-019002 A
Plaintiff,	
v.	QUESTIONNAIRE FOR PROSPECTIVE JURORS
ROBERT DONALD LEMKE,	(Honorable Douglas Rayes)
Defendant.	

Your name has been drawn as a prospective juror in this criminal case. The questions on this form are designed to help the court and the lawyers learn something about your background and your views on issues that may be related to this case. Its use will avoid the necessity of asking each prospective juror every one of these questions in open court. This should help to shorten the jury selection process for everyone. The questions are asked not to invade your privacy, but to make sure that you can be a fair and impartial juror. If there is any reason why you might not be able to give both sides a fair trial in this case, it is important that you say so.

All information contained in this questionnaire will be kept confidential. It will be reviewed only by the judge, the attorneys in the case and their staff. Neither your identities nor your answers will be released to the general public or the media.

Please respond to each question as fully and completely as possible. Your complete honesty is necessary, so that both the prosecution and the defense will have a meaningful opportunity to select a fair and impartial jury. Because this questionnaire is part of the jury selection process, the questionnaires are to be answered under your oath as a prospective juror to tell the truth. You are instructed not to discuss this case or the questionnaire with anyone, including your family and fellow jurors. It is important that your answers be your own.

If you need more space for your responses, or wish to make further comments about any of your answers, please use the extra sheets that are attached to the back of your questionnaires. Please keep in mind that there are no "right" or "wrong" answers, only complete and incomplete answers. Complete answers are far more helpful than incomplete answers. They assist all parties in obtaining a fair and impartial jury.

The questions contained in this questionnaire are intended only to provide the Court and the parties with information about you and your views. The fact that a particular question is asked does not imply that the subject of the question is issue in this case. As you read the questions, you should not draw any inferences about the issues which will be decided in this case.

Do not leave any questions blank. If a question does not apply to you in any way, please write "N/A" (not applicable) rather than leaving the question blank. If you feel that the answer to a question would be too personal, please say so in the space provided. You will have the opportunity to discuss your answer privately, with only the judge and lawyers in the case.

JUROR QUESTIONNAIRE

1. Name _____

   Juror Number (assigned by the Court)_____

2. Age: _____ Sex: _____

3. Area in which you live (not a specific address): _____

4. Place of Birth:_____

5. Marital status:
   _____ Single and never married
   _____ Currently married and have been for_____years
   _____ Single, but married in the past for_____years
   _____ Single, but living with a partner for_____years
   _____ Widowed, but married in the past for_____years
   _____ Other:_____
   Any prior marriages?   Yes____ No____
   If yes, how many? _____

6. What is the last level of education you completed?
   _____ Grade school or less   _____ Some college
   _____ Some high school   _____ College graduate
   _____ High school graduate   _____ Post graduate work
   _____ Technical or business school

7. Please name the schools and colleges you attended,
   your major areas of study and list any degrees you may have.

   _____

   _____

8. a. Other educational programs (vocational schools, night schools, part-time study, certificate programs) you attended:

_____

_____

   b. What special training skills do you have? (Please include any technical, medical, psychology or scientific training and special skills acquired on-the-job.)

_____

_____

9. Do you still attend or do you plan to attend school?   Yes____ No____
   If Yes, what do you or will you study?

_____

10. Please name the schools and colleges you attended, your major areas of study, and list any degrees you may have.

_____

_____

11. a. Other educational programs (vocational schools, night schools, part-time study, certificate programs) you attended:

_____

_____

    b. What special training skills do you have? (Please include any technical, medical, psychology or scientific training and special skills acquired on-the-job.)

_____

_____

12. Current employment status:
    ___ Employed full-time   ___ Unemployed - looking for work
    ___ Employed part-time   ___ Unemployed - not looking for work
    ___ Homemaker   ___ Retired
    ___ Student   ___ Disabled

13. What is your occupation (or what was it, if retired or unemployed?)

_____

   a. By whom are (were) you employed? _____

   b. What are (were) your specific duties and responsibilities
      on the job? _____

_____

   c. How long have (did) you work(ed) there? _____

14. Please list the general types of jobs you have had or work you have
    done as an adult.

_____

15. Current employment status of spouse: (If widowed, divorced
    or separated, please complete the following questions as to your
    most recent spouse/mate.)

   ___Employed full-time   ___Unemployed—looking for work
   ___Employed part-time   ___Unemployed—not looking for work
   ___Homemaker   ___Retired
   ___Student   ___Disabled

16. a. What is his/her occupation (or what was it, if retired or
      unemployed?)

_____

  b. By whom is (was) he/she employed?

_____

17. What is the last level of education he/she completed?
     _____ Grade school or less   _____ Some college
     _____ Some high school   _____ College graduate
     _____ High school graduate _____ Post graduate work
     _____ Technical or business school

18. Have you, or any member of your family, or any close friends been associated with or employed by any law enforcement agency? YES _____ NO _____ . If YES, describe it briefly and, if other than yourself, state the relationship of the person to you:

_____

_____

19. Have you or anyone close to you ever worked for, applied to or had training with: (Check all that apply)

_____ a. Any law enforcement, security or investigative agency?

_____ b. A prison, jail, detention center or probation service?

_____ c. Any city or town attorney, Attorney General, state or federal prosecutor or court?

_____ d. Any law firm that practices defense of those investigated for or accused of crimes?

_____ e. A psychologist, psychiatrist, mental health center, mental hospital, social work or social service agency or counseling service?

_____ f. Medical, nursing, or EMT services?

_____ g. A treatment program for alcohol, drug, or any other substance abuse?

20. Do you, or any members of your family, or close friends, to your knowledge have any background or training in the investigation of civil or criminal matters? YES _____ NO _____ . If YES, describe it briefly and, if other than yourself, state the relationship of the person to you:

_____

_____

21. Do you, or any member of your family, or close friends, to your knowledge have any background or training in any other field involved in the criminal justice system, for example, probation, parole, Department of Corrections or Court work? YES _____ NO _____ . If YES, describe it briefly and, if other than yourself, state the relationship of the person to you:

_____

_____

22. Do you feel that you or someone close to you has been treated unfairly in the past by someone in law enforcement, or by a prosecutor, or by a court? YES _____ NO _____ If YES, briefly describe the event(s):

_____

23. Brief summary of the case: On August 8, 2002, Rick Chance, a local businessman and spokesman for Empire Glass was shot and killed in a Tempe hotel. Brandi Hungerford admitted participation in this incident, and is expected to testify in Robert Lemke's trial. Do you recognize the names of any of the following (Please circle the names you recognize):

Detective John Ferrin, Tempe P.D.   Candess Hunter
Detective Steven Stadel, Tempe P.D.   Mary Miller
Detective John McGowan, Tempe P.D.   Fred Pratt
Detective Todd Bailey, Tempe P.D.   Gillian Moore
Detective Tom Magazzini, Tempe P.D.   Brandi Hungerford
Detective Larry Baggs, Tempe P.D.   Brad Edwards
Detective Susan Schoville, Tempe P.D.   Dan Olson
Sergeant Mark Perkovich, Tempe P.D.   David Lewis
Detective Trent Luckow, Tempe P.D.
Detective Tom O'Brien, Tempe P.D.
Detective Kyle Schmidt, Tempe P.D.
Tech. Lynette Corning, Tempe P.D.
Lisa Peloza, DPS
Scott Milne, DPS
Dr. Phillip Keen, Medical Examiner
Detective Brian Vold, Tacoma P.D.
Detective Ed Baker, Tacoma P.D.
Lieutenant Stewart, Pierce County Sheriff's Office
Ramona Dedden, Pierce County Sheriff's Office
Kevin Stock, Pierce County Court

Describe briefly the nature of your association or acquaintance with the person(s) whose name(s) you have circled and/or the reason you recognize the name(s).

_____
_____
_____

24. Based upon the limited information you have regarding this case, does this case sound familiar to you? YES _____ NO _____

Have you seen, heard or read anything about this case from any source? YES _____ NO _____

If YES, state the source of your information and the approximate number of times you have seen, heard or read anything about this case (e.g., newspaper, radio, TV, conversation.) Include any conversations you may have overheard.

_____

_____

_____

25. Describe anything you may know or remember about the case. Please be as complete as possible.

_____

_____

_____

26. Have you watched crime shows on television that depict police officers, prosecutors, defense attorneys, and/or trials? YES _____ NO _____

If YES, which ones?

_____

_____

27. Do you feel these television shows are realistic portrayals of the criminal justice system? YES _____ NO _____
Please explain:_____

_____

28. There will be DNA testimony in this case. What personal knowledge, experience, beliefs or opinions do you have about DNA evidence?

_____

_____

THREE PHASES IN CAPITAL TRIALS

Robert Lemke is charged with First Degree Murder. After the jury is selected, the jury will start the first phase of possibly a three phase trial process. The first phase is called the "guilty/not-guilty" phase. Depending on the jury's verdict in the first phase, there may be a second phase called the "aggravation factor" phase of the trial. Depending on the jury's verdicts in the aggravation factor phase trial, there may be a third phase called the "penalty phase trial."

I will now give you a brief outline of the procedures involving these three possible phases. At all three phases, if they occur, you will receive further and more detailed instructions, so you do not have to commit them to memory now.

(1) Guilty/Not Guilty Trial

In the first, guilty/not-guilty phase trial, the jury will be asked to decide whether the State has proven that the Defendant committed First Degree Murder as alleged by the State beyond a reasonable doubt. The Defendant is presumed to be innocent of the charge. The State must convince each juror of the Defendant's guilt of First Degree Murder beyond a reasonable doubt.

If the jury finds the Defendant not guilty of First Degree Murder, then the next two phases of the trial will not occur.

If the jury finds the Defendant guilty of First Degree Murder, then the trial would proceed to a second phase, called the "Aggravation Factor" phase.

(2) Aggravation Factor Phase

At the "aggravation factor" phase of the trial, the jury will be asked to determine whether or not a specified aggravating factor alleged by the State is true beyond a reasonable doubt. The State must convince each juror that the aggravating factor alleged has been proven beyond a reasonable doubt.

If you determine the State has not proven an aggravating factor beyond a reasonable doubt, then the next possible phase of the trial will not occur. If you determine the State has proven an aggravating factor beyond a reasonable doubt, then the "penalty phase" of the trial will be held.

(3) Penalty Phase Trial

At the "penalty phase" of the trial, the jury will be asked to determine if specified mitigating circumstances exist, and whether or not a death sentence is the appropriate sentence.

In determining whether to impose a sentence of death, each individual juror shall take into account the aggravating circumstances that all the jurors have found to be proven and take into account any mitigating circumstances that each individual juror has found to be proven.

Each juror will then have to determine whether there is mitigation that is sufficiently substantial to call for leniency. The jury will then decide whether the death penalty is the appropriate sentence. The decision to impose the death penalty is not a recommendation. Your decision will be binding on the judge.

If the jury determines that the death penalty is not the appropriate sentence, then the defendant will be sentenced to life imprisonment and it will be up to the judge to decide whether the sentence of life imprisonment shall be life without parole or life with the possibility of parole after serving 25 years imprisonment.

29. What is your opinion of the death penalty?

_____

_____

30. For this question, assume Arizona does not have the death penalty. If there were a referendum on the next ballot to enact a death penalty, how would you vote? Explain. _____

_____

31. Do you believe you can put aside your personal views on the death penalty and apply the law given to you by the Court, if doing so would result in the death of the defendant in this case? YES _____ NO _____

32. Do you have any personal, moral, religious, philosophical or conscientious objections to the imposition of the death penalty? YES _____ NO _____ If your answer is "YES," please explain.

_____

_____

33. Are your views regarding the death penalty, whether based on moral, philosophical, religious or any other grounds, so strongly held by you so that you will be prevented or substantially impaired from performing your sworn duty to follow the law and applying it to the facts of this case? YES _____ NO _____ If your answer is "YES," please explain.

_____

_____

34. Will you, for whatever reason, automatically vote against the death penalty without considering the evidence and the instructions of law that will be presented to you? YES _____ NO _____
If your answer is "YES," please explain.

_____

_____

35. Conversely, will you, for whatever reason, automatically vote for the death penalty without considering the evidence and the instructions of law that will be presented to you? YES _____ NO _____
If your answer is "YES," please explain.

_____

_____

36. Is there any member of your household, close relative or friend who is opposed to the death penalty to the extent that you would feel uncomfortable or under any kind of pressure in deciding the defendant's fate? YES _____ NO _____
If your answer is "YES," please explain.

_____

_____

37. Have you ever personally known anyone who was killed other than by accident? YES _____ NO _____
If your answer is "YES," please explain.

_____

_____

_____

38. Have you or an immediate family member or close friend ever killed anyone, accidentally or otherwise? YES _____ NO _____
If your answer is "YES," please explain.

_____

39. If you determine that the appropriate sentence is life, the judge will determine if the sentence will be life without the possibility of parole or life with the possibility of parole only after at least 25 years have been served. Do you disagree with the law that requires the judge to make the decision about which type of life sentence to impose? YES _____ NO _____ If your answer is "YES," please explain.

_____

40. The cost of either form of sentence cannot be considered by the jury in deciding punishment. What do you think of this law?

_____

_____

41. Do you feel that the death penalty is imposed either too often or too seldom? YES _____ NO _____
If YES, please explain:

_____

_____

42. Do you belong to any group that advocates either the increased use or the elimination of the death penalty? YES _____ NO _____
If YES, please describe the group and the extent of your participation:

_____

_____

43. You will be instructed that the jurors must accept and follow the law as instructed by the judge, whether or not you personally agree with that law. Are you willing to follow this rule of law? YES _____ NO _____
If NO, please explain:

_____

_____

_____

44. If the jury finds the defendant guilty of First Degree Murder and finds that at least one aggravating factor has been proven, the Court will instruct the jury that if the jury unanimously finds that either (1) there is no mitigation or (2) that the mitigation is not sufficiently substantial to call for leniency, the jury must vote to impose the death penalty. Likewise, the jury will be instructed that if the jury unanimously finds that there is mitigation sufficiently substantial to call for leniency, the jury must vote to impose a life sentence. Do you believe that you could follow an instruction of law that imposes either of these requirements? YES _____ NO _____ If NO, please explain:

_____

_____

45. Mitigation evidence includes any aspect of the defendant's life, character or record and any circumstance of the offense that is a basis for a sentence less than death. What is your opinion of mitigation evidence?

_____

46. The law requires that aggravating factors be proven beyond a reasonable doubt. Mitigation, on the other hand, need only be proven by a preponderance of the evidence, Do you agree with this law? YES _____ NO _____ Can you follow this law even if you disagree with it? YES _____ NO _____ Please explain your answers to the above.

_____

47. The law allows only a very few and very specific aggravating factors to be used, if proven beyond a reasonable doubt and not overcome by mitigation, to support the state's request for a death sentence. No other fact or detail about the case or the person accused may be considered as an aggravating factor. Do you agree with this law? YES _____ NO _____ Can you follow this law even if you disagree with it? YES _____ NO _____ Please explain your answer to the above.

_____

_____

48. The law puts absolutely no restrictions on what can be considered mitigation. Do you agree with this law? YES _____ NO _____
Can you follow this law even if you disagree with it? YES _____ NO _____
Please explain your answer to the above.

_____

_____

_____

49. Are there are any matters not covered by this questionnaire that should be discussed regarding your ability to serve on this jury?
YES _____ NO _____ If YES, please explain:

_____

_____

_____

Appendix 3

JUROR OATHS

FINAL JURY

You (and each of you) do solemnly swear that you will give careful attention to the proceedings, abide by the Court's instructions, and render a verdict in accordance with the law and evidence presented to you, so help you God?

Appendix 4

JURORS

1—Debbie (Alternate)
2—Mike
3—Linda
4—Owen (Alternate)
5—Nick (Alternate)
6—Ginny
7—Pete (Alterate)
8—Francie
9—Betty
10—Ellie
11—Kathy
12—Abby
13—Ivy
14—Christie
15—Jackie
16—Holly

Appendix 5

PRELIMINARY JURY INSTRUCTIONS

1. INTRODUCTION TO PRELIMINARY INSTRUCTIONS

Now that we are about to begin the trial, I would like to explain to you what will happen during the trial. In addition, I have some rules about your conduct during the trial.

It is your duty to follow these instructions. These instructions are preliminary only. After you have heard all of the evidence I will read to you the final instructions of law. You will also receive a written copy. You must follow the final instructions in deciding the case.

It will be your duty, and no one else's, to decide the facts. You must decide the facts only from the evidence produced in court. You must not speculate or guess about any fact. You must not be influenced by sympathy or prejudice.

You will hear the evidence, decide the facts, and then apply those facts to the law I will give to you at the end of the trial. That is how you will reach your verdict.

Please do not take anything I may say or do during the trial as indicating any opinion you may feel I have about the facts. You, and you alone, are the judges of the facts.

2. IMPORTANCE OF JURY SERVICE

Jury service is an important part of our system of justice, with a long and distinguished tradition in western civilization. From its beginning, American law has viewed the jury system as an effective means of drawing on the collective wisdom, experience, and fact-finding abilities of persons such as yourselves. While it may be an occasional inconvenience, jury service is an important responsibility for you, one which I am sure you will take seriously.

The law provides for a jury of eight (8) persons or twelve (12) persons, depending on the type of case. We have more than that number so that, if a juror becomes ill or has a personal emergency, the trial can continue without that juror,

At the end of the case, if more than the required number of jurors remains, a random drawing will determine alternates in open court. Please do not be concerned with who may or may not be selected as an alternate juror at the end of the case.

3. NOTE TAKING PERMITTED

At the end of the trial you will have to make your decision based on what you recall of the evidence. You will not be given a written transcript of any testimony; you should pay close attention to the testimony as it is given.

Notebooks and pens have been provided for note taking. No juror is required to take notes. Some of you may feel that note taking is not helpful because it may interfere with the hearing and evaluation of evidence. For example, you need to watch witnesses during their testimony in order to assess their appearance, behavior, memory and whatever else bears on their believability.

Notes are only to help you remember. They should not take the place of your independent memory of the testimony. On the other hand, if you take no notes at all, you run the risk of forgetting important testimony needed for your verdict.

Please remember the number on the cover of your notebook so that it can be identified as yours after each recess. For longer recesses (overnight and weekends) the Bailiff will store the notebooks and return them to you when the trial resumes. At no time will anyone but you open or read your notebooks.

Please do not be influenced at all by my taking notes at times. What I write down may have nothing to do with what you will be concerned with at this trial.

At the end of the case your notes will be collected, not read, but destroyed by the Bailiff, unless you choose to take the notes with you.

4. ORDER OF TRIAL—GUILT / INNOCENCE PHASE

Trials generally proceed in the following order:

First, the prosecutor will make an opening statement giving a preview of the case.

Second, the defendant's attorney may, but is not required to make an opening statement outlining the defense case. If defendant decides to make an opening statement, it may be made either immediately after the prosecutor's statement or it may be postponed until after the State's case has been presented. What is said in opening statements is not evidence nor is it an argument. The purpose of an opening statement is to help you prepare for anticipated evidence.

Third, the State will present its evidence.

Fourth, after the prosecutor finishes, the defendant may present evidence. The defendant is not required to produce evidence.

Fifth, if the defendant does produce evidence, the State may present additional, or rebuttal, evidence.

Sixth, after all the evidence is in, I read and give you copies of the final instructions, the rules of law you must follow in reaching your verdict.

Seventh, the attorneys will make closing arguments to tell you what they think the evidence shows and how they think you should decide the case. The prosecutor has the right to open and close the argument because the State has the burden of proof. Just as in opening statements, what is said in closing arguments is not evidence.

Eighth, you will deliberate in the jury room about the evidence and rules of law and decide upon a verdict. Once you reach it, the verdict will be read in court with you and the parties present.

5. CONDUCT OF JURORS (ADMONITION)

There are a number of important rules governing your own conduct during the trial, Sometimes these are called admonitions.

First, you should keep an open mind throughout the trial and reach your conclusion only after you have heard all the evidence, the final instructions of law and the closing argurnents of counsel. Form your opinions only after you have had an opportunity to discuss the case with each other in the jury room at the end of the trial.

Second, do not discuss the case during the trial, either among yourselves or with anyone else. In a civil case, the jurors are permitted to discuss the evidence during the trial while the trial progresses. In a criminal case such as this, however, the jurors are not permitted to discuss the evidence until all the evidence has been presented and the jurors have retired to deliberate on the verdict. You therefore may not discuss the evidence among yourselves until you retire to deliberate on your verdict. Avoid overhearing others discussing the case. If you happen to overhear another person you might hear information the parties do not learn about and are unabte to prove wrong or explain. To minimize the risk of accidentally overhearing something about the case, I ask that you wear the juror's badge while in and around the courthouse. Should you overhear a discussion, report that fact at once to any member of the staff.

Third, though it is entirely natural to talk or visit with people with whom you are thrown in contact, please do not talk with any of the attorneys, defendant, witnesses, or spectators either in or out of the courtroom. If you meet in the hallways or elevators, there is nothing wrong with saying a "good morning" or "good afternoon," but your conversation should end there. In no other way can the parties be assured of the absolute fairness they are entitled to expect from you as jurors. If the attorneys, parties and witnesses do not greet you outside of court, or avoid riding in the same elevator with you, they are not being rude. They are just carefully observing this rule forbidding contact.

Fourth, because this case involves events that occurred at a particular location, you may be tempted to visit the scene. Please do not do so. Important changes may have occurred at the location since the original event. In making an unguided visit without the benefit of an explanation, you might get an erroneous or partial impression.

Last, do not attempt any tests, experiments or other investigation on your own. It would be difficult to impossible to duplicate conditions shown by the evidence; therefore, your results would not be reliable. In any event, your verdict must be based solely upon the evidence produced in this courtroom.

Before any break or recess I shall not repeat these admonitions word for word. I will simply say, "Please remember the admonition." The rules apply at all times during the trial—24 hours a day, 7 days a week—until you return a verdict in open court and are discharged by me.

6. FUNCTIONS OF A JURY

As jurors, you have two major duties:

First, you must listen to and look at the evidence and decide from the evidence what the facts of this case are. It is your job, and no one else's, to decide what the facts are. You will decide the credibility and weight to be given to any evidence presented in the case, whether it be direct or circumstantial evidence. I will endeavor to preside impartially and not express any opinion concerning the facts. Any views of mine on the facts are totally irrelevant. This includes gestures or frowns or smiles or other body language. Comments to or questions of lawyers or witnesses by me are intended to move the case along or to clarify some evidence.

Second, you must carefully listen to the laws that I will instruct you on at the end of the case. It is your duty to follow them in reaching your verdict.

In fulfilling your duties as jurors you must not be influenced by feelings of sympathy, bias or prejudice.

7. EVIDENCE, STATEMENTS OF LAWYERS, AND RULINGS

As I mentioned earlier, it is your job to decide from the evidence what the facts are. Here are eight rules that will help you decide what is and what is not evidence:

1. Evidence to be considered: You are to determine the facts only from the testimony of witnesses and from exhibits received in evidence. You will decide the credibility and weight to be given to any evidence presented in the case. All exhibits received in evidence will be made available to you in the jury room during deliberations. The evidence you will hear and consider will be that which is permitted by our laws and rules of evidence.

2. Direct and Circumstantial Evidence: Evidence may be direct or circumstantial. Direct evidence is the testimony of a witness who saw, heard, or otherwise observed an event, Circumstantial evidence is the proof of a fact or facts from which you may find another fact. The law makes no distinction between direct and circumstantial evidence. It is for you to determine the importance to be given to the evidence, regardless of whether it is direct or circumstantial.

3. Lawyer's statements: Ordinarily, statements or arguments made by the

lawyers in the case are not evidence. Their purpose is to help you understand the evidence and law. However, if the lawyers agree or stiputate that some particular fact is true, you should accept it as the truth.

4. Questions to a witnesss: By itself, a question is not evidence. A question can only be used to give meaning to a witness's answer.

5. Objections to questions: If a lawyer objects to a question and I do not allow the witness to answer, you must not try to guess what the answer might have been. You must also not try to guess the reason why the lawyer objected in the first place.

6. Rejected evidence: At times during the trial, testimony or exhibits will be offered as evidence but I might not allow them to become evidence. Because they never become evidence, you must not consider them.

7. Stricken evidence: At times I may order some evidence to be stricken, or thrown out. Because what is stricken is no longer in evidence, you must not consider it.

8. Limiting instructions: At times I may instruct that evidence is admitted for a limited purpose. Consider the evidence only for that limited purpose.

9. Bench Conferences: At times there may be a need for me to talk with the lawyers at the bench to resolve disputes. You will not be able to hear our conference. This enables us to resolve disputes without taking a break in the proceedings. If we sent you to the jury room every time we needed to have a discussion outside of your presence, it would take considerable time and delay the proceedings. Please don't be concerned with what we may be discussing at our bench conference.

8. CREDIBILITY OF WITNESSES

In deciding the facts of this case, you should consider what testimony to accept, and what to reject. You may accept everything a witness says, or part of it, or none of it.

In evaluating testimony, you should use the tests for accuracy and truthfulness that people use in determining matters of importance in everyday life, including such factors as the witness's abitity to see, hear, or know the things the witness testified about; the quality of the witness's memory; the witness's manner while testifying; whether the witness has any motive, bias, or prejudice; whether the witness is contradicted by anything the witness said or wrote before trial, or by other evidence; and, the reasonableness of the witness's testimony when considered in the light of the other evidence.

Consider all of the evidence in light of reason, common sense, and experience.

9. QUESTIONS BY JURORS

If at any time you have difficulty hearing or seeing something that you should be hearing or seeing, or if you get into personal distress for any reason, raise your hand and let me know.

If you have any questions about parking, restaurants, or other personal matters relating to jury service, feel free to ask the Bailiff or any of the court staff. But remember that the Admonition applies to them, as it does to everyone else; so do not try to discuss the case with court staff.

During the course of the trial, you may wish to ask questions of witnesses who testify. You may do so using the following procedure:

After counsel has examined each witness, I will ask members of the jury whether any of you have any questions for the witness. Please remember that you are under no obligation to ask questions. Both counsel know the case better than you or I do, and each of them will be attempting to place before you all the evidence needed to assist you in reaching a proper verdict.

If you have a question, please write it down on the form provided. Do not put your name or juror number on the question. The questions must be directed to the witness and not to the lawyers or the judge. The purpose of a question is to clarify the evidence that has been presented, not to explore theories of your own or to discredit a witness.

Do not discuss your questions with other jurors.

The Bailiff will collect the questions and I will then consider whether they are permitted under our rules of evidence and relevant to the subject matter of the witness's testimony. I will also discuss them with counsel.

If the court determines that the question may be properly asked, I will then read the question to the witness.

It is important to understand that rejection of a proposed question because it is not within the rules of evidence or because it is not relevant is no reflection upon you. Also, if a particular question cannot be asked of the witness, you must not speculate about what the answer might have been.

10. A CHARGE IS NOT EVIDENCE

The State has charged the defendant with certain crimes. A charge is not evidence against the defendant. You must not think the defendant is guilty just because of the charge. The defendant has pled "not guilty." The plea of "not guilty" means that the State must prove each element of the charge beyond a reasonable doubt.

11. PRESUMPTION OF INNOCENCE AND BURDEN OF PROOF

The law does not require a defendant to prove innocence. Every defendant is presumed by law to be innocent.

The State has the burden of proving the defendant guilty beyond a reasonable doubt. The State must prove each element of the charge beyond a reasonable doubt. In civil cases, it is only necessary to prove that a fact is more likely true than not or that its truth is highly probable. In criminal cases such as this, the State's proof must be more powerful than that. It must be beyond a reasonable doubt.

Proof beyond a reasonable doubt is proof that leaves you firmly convinced of the defendant's guilt. There are very few things in this world that we know with absolute certainty, and in criminal cases the law does not require proof that overcomes every doubt. If, based on your consideration of the evidence, you are firmly convinced that the defendant is guilty of the crime charged, you must find him guilty. If, on the other hand, you think there is a real possibility that he is not guilty, you must give him the benefit of the doubt and find him not guilty.

12. EXCLUSION OF WITNESSES

The rule of exclusion of witnesses is in effect and will be observed by all the witnesses until the trial is over and a result announced. This means that all witnesses will remain outside the courtroom during the entire trial except when one is called to the witness stand. They will wait in the areas directed by the Bailiff.

The rule also forbids witnesses from telling anyone but the lawyers what they will testify about or what they have testified to. If witnesses do talk to the lawyers about their testimony, other witnesses and jurors should avoid being present or overhearing.

The defendant may remain in the courtroom at all times whether or not called as a witness. In addition, the State may choose a person, such as an officer or investigator, to assist by sitting with the State during the trial.

The lawyers are directed to inform all other witnesses of these rules and to remind them of their obligations from time to time as may be necessary. The parties and their lawyers should keep a careful lookout to prevent any potential witness from remaining in the courtroom if they inadvertently enter.

13. SCHEDULING DURING TRIAL

We will all do our best to move the case along, but delays frequently occur. These won't be anyone's fault, so don't hold them against the parties. Delays usually occur because the attorneys and I need to resolve certain legal matters before these matters may be presented to you or because I am busy with emergency matters in other cases.

The usual hours of trial will be from 10:30 a.m. to 4:30 p.m. Unless a different starting time is announced prior to recessing for the evening, you may assume a starting time of 10:30 a.m. for the next day.

At the beginning of the day, please assemble according to the instructions given to you by the Baitiff. Please do not come back into the courtroom until the Baitiff calls upon you.

14. MEDIA COVERAGE

There may or may not be news media coverage of the trial. What the news media covers is up to them. If there is media coverage, you must avoid it during the trial. If you do encounter something about this case in the news media during the trial, end your exposure to it immediately and report it to me as soon as you can.

If there are cameras in the courtroom during the trial, do not be concerned about them. Court rules require that the proceedings be photographed or televised in such a way that no juror can be recognized.

15. EMERGENCY FIRE AND EVACUATION PROCEDURES

The Baillff will instruct you on all emergency evacuation procedures as well as all other aspects of what would be expected of you during any emergency situation.

16. CONCLUSION OF PRELIMINARY INSTRUCTIONS

The rules of law I have shared with you in the past few minutes are preliminary only. At the end of the case I will read to you and give you a copy of the final instructions of law. In deciding the case you must be guided by the final instructions.

Appendix 5.1

TRIAL DAYS

Week 1:   Monday August 15 through Friday August 19
          10:30 a.m. start — 5 days

Week 2:   Monday August 22 through Thursday August 25
          10:30 a.m. start — 4 days

Week 3:   Monday August 29 through Wednesday August 31
          10:30 a.m. start — 3 days

Week 4:   Tuesday September 6 through Thursday September 8
          10:30 a.m. start — 3 days

Week 5:   Monday September 12 through Thursday September 15
          10:30 a.m. start — 4 days

Week 6:   Monday September 19 through Thursday September 22
          10:30 a.m. start — 4 days

Appendix 6

QUESTIONS BY JURORS

Question 1:
> How much force would be required to make the bruising on the victim's head?

Question 2:
> Brad mentioned he was taking Mr. Lemke to get a rental car to go back to Phoenix. Didn't Mary state Lemke was going to drive her Civic back?

Question 3: (NOT ASKED)
> Were any fingerprints found on any items in room? If so, whose?

Question 4:
> By position of body on floor could victim have been sitting on the bed?

Question 5: (NOT ASKED THIS WITNESS)
> Clarification—Is Area Code 253 a Tacoma, Washington Area Code? If not, where?

Question 6:
> Where did bullet in box come from?

Question 7:
> What relevant phone numbers did Robert Lemke call from the jail?

Question 8:
> What was the time of call to Dan and duration of call?

Question 9:
Where was key to padlock on gun case?

Question 10:
Was the phone number that Brandi received from Robert the same phone number that Rick gave Brandi on their second encounter?

Question 11:
Did you let Robert Lemke into hotel on Aughst 8th or in any way open an outside door for him?

Question 12: (NOT ASKED)
On your prior convictions, what were the charges and were any of the charges similar to what you are being charged with in this case. If so, was the mode of operation similar to the robbery charge in this case?

Question 13:
Did you ever call Mim? Did you have her phone number?

Question 14:
Did you know name of restaurant where Mim worked?

Question 15:
Why didn't you ask Brandi what was going on the night she came over on August 8?

Question 16: (NOT ASKED)
Did you relate the facts you stated today to police when arrested in 2002?

Appendix 7

FINAL JURY INSTRUCTIONS
GUILT PHASE

State
v.
ROBERT DONALD LEMKE
CR2002-019002 A

Duty of Jury

It is your duty as a juror to decide this case by applying these jury instructions to the facts as you determine them. You must follow these jury instructions. They are the rules you should use to decide this case.

It is your duty to determine what the facts are in the case by determining what actually happened. Determine the facts only from the evidence produced in court. When I say evidence, I mean the testimony of witnesses and the exhibits introduced in court. You should not guess about any fact. You must not be influenced by sympathy or prejudice. You must not be concerned with any opinion that you feel I have about the facts. You, as jurors, are the sole judges of what happened.

You must consider all these instructions. Do not pick out one instruction, or part of one, and ignore the others. As you determine the facts, however, you may find that some instructions no longer apply. You must then consider the instructions that do apply, together with the facts as you have determined them.

Lawyers' Comments Are Not Evidence

In their opening statements and closing arguments, the lawyers have talked to you about the law and the evidence. What the lawyers said is not evidence, but it may help you to understand the law and the evidence.

Stipulations

The lawyers are permitted to stipulate that certain facts exist. This means that both sides agree those facts do exist and are part of the evidence.

Evidence To Be Considered

You are to determine what the facts in the case are from the evidence produced in court. If the court sustained an objection to a lawyer's question, you must disregard it and any answer given.

Any testimony stricken from the court record must not be considered.

Indictment Is Not Evidence

The State has charged the defendant with certain crimes. A charge is not evidence against the defendant. You must not think that the defendant is guilty just because of a charge. The defendant has pled "not guilty." This plea of "not guilty" means that the State must prove each element of the charge beyond a reasonable doubt.

Burden of Proof

The law does not require a defendant to prove innocence. Every defendant is presumed by law to be innocent.

The State has the burden of proving the defendant guilty beyond a reasonable doubt. In civil cases, it is only necessary to prove that a fact is more likely true than not or that its truth is highly probable. In criminal cases such as this, the State's proof must be more powerful than that. It must be beyond a reasonable doubt.

Proof beyond a reasonable doubt is proof that leaves you firmly convinced of the defendant's guilt. There are very few things in this world that we know with absolute certainty, and in criminal cases the law does not require proof that overcomes every doubt. If, based on your consideration of the evidence, you are firmly convinced that the defendant is guilty of the crime charged, you must find him guilty. If on the other hand, you think there is a real possibility that he is not guilty, you must give him the benefit of the doubt and find him not guilty.

Evidence of Any Kind

The State must prove guilt beyond a reasonable doubt with its own evidence. The deFendant is not required to produce evidence of any kind. The decision on whether to produce any evidence is left to the defendant acting with the advice of an attorney. The defendant's failure to produce any evidence is not evidence of guilt.

Credibility of Witnesses

In determining the evidence, you must decide whether to believe the witnesses and their testimony. As you do this, you should consider the testimony in light of all the other evidence in the case. This means you may consider such things as the witnesses' ability and opportunity to observe, their manner and memory while testifying, any motive or prejudice they might have, and any inconsistent statements they may have made.

Defendant's Testimony

You must evaluate the defendant's testimony the same as any witness' testimony.

Credibility of Felon as Defendant Witness

You have heard evidence that the defendant has previously been convicted of a criminal offense. You may consider that evidence only as it may affect the defendant's believability as a witness. You must not consider a prior conviction as evidence of guilt of the crime for which the defendant is now on trial.

Credibility of Witness

You have heard evidence that a witness has been convicted of a criminal offense. You may consider this evidence only as it may affect the witness' believability.

"Intentionally" or "With Intent To" Defined

"Intentionally" or "with intent to" means that a defendant's objective is to cause that result or to engage in that conduct.

"Knowingly" Defined

"Knowingly" means that a defendant acted with awareness of or belief in the existence of conduct or circumstances constituting an offense. It does not mean that a defendant must have known that the conduct is forbidden by law.

Included Mental States—Knowingly

If the State is required to prove that the defendant acted "knowingly," that requirement is satisfied if the State proves that the defendant acted "intentionally."

"Recklessly" or "Reckless Disregard" Defined

"Recklessly" or "reckless disregard" means that a defendant is aware of and consciously disregards a substantial and unjustifiable risk that the result will occur or that the circumstance exists. The risk must be such that disregarding it is a gross deviation from what a reasonable person would do in the situation.

Accomplice

A person is criminally accountable for the conduct of another if the person is an accomplice of such other person in the commission of the offense.

An accomplice is a person who, with the intent to promote or facilitate the commission of an offense either:

(1) Solicits or commands another person to commit the offense; or

(2) Aids, counsels, agrees to aid or attempts to aid another person in planning or committing the offense; or

(3) Provides means or opportunity to another person to commit the offense.

In the prosecution of an accomplice, it is no defense that the other person has not been prosecuted for or convicted of such offense or has an immunity to prosecution for such offense.

Mere Presence

The mere presence of a defendant at the scene of a crime, together with knowledge a crime is being committed, is insufficient to establish guilt.

Testimony of Law Enforcement Officers

The testimony of a law enforcement officer is not entitled to any greater or lesser importance or believability merely because of the fact that the witness is a law enforcement officer. You are to consider the testimony of a police officer just as you would the testimony of any other witness.

Separate Counts

Each count charges a separate and distinct offense. You must decide each count separately on the evidence with the law applicable to it, uninfluenced by your decision on any other count. You may find that the State has proved beyond a reasonable doubt, all, some, or none of the charged offenses. Your finding for each count must be stated in a separate verdict.

Jury Not To Consider Penalty

You must decide whether the defendant is guilty or not guilty by determining what the facts in the case are and applying these jury instructions. You must not consider the possible punishment when deciding on guilt.

Evidence of Defendant's Non-Presence

The state has the burden of proving that the defendant was present at the time and place the alleged crime was committed. If you have a reasonable doubt whether the defendant was present at the time and place the alleged crime was committed, you must find the defendant not guilty.

Voluntary Act

Before you may convict the defendant of the charged crimes, you must find that the State proved beyond a reasonable doubt that the defendant committed a voluntary act. A voluntary act means a bodily movement performed consciously and as a result of effort and determination. You must consider all the evidence in deciding whether the defendant committed the act voluntarily.

Direct and Circumstantial Evidence

Evidence may be direct or circumstantial. Direct evidence is the testimony of a witness who saw, heard, or otherwise observed an event. Circumstantial evidence is the proof of a fact or facts from which you may find another fact. The law makes no distinction between direct and circumstantial evidence. It is for you to determine the importance to be given to the evidence, regardless of whether it is direct or circumstantial.

Expert Testimony

A witness may give an opinion on a subject upon which the witness has become an expert because of education, study, or experience. You should consider the opinion of an expert and the reasons, if any, given for it. However, you are not bound by any expert opinion. Give the expert opinion the importance that you believe it deserves.

First Degree Murder

The crime of first degree murder requires proof of the following two things:
1. The defendant committed armed robbery; *and*
2. In the course of and in furtherance of this crime or immediate flight from this crime, the defendant or another person caused the death of any person.

Conspiracy to Commit Armed Robbery

The crime of Conspiracy to Commit Armed Robbery requires proof of the following things:

1. That the defendant agreed with one or more persons that one of them or another person would engage in certain conduct; *and*

2. That the defendant intended to promote or assist the commission of such conduct; *and*

3. That the intended conduct would constitute the crime of Armed Robbery.

The indictment charges the defendant with Conspiracy to Commit Armed Robbery and the crime of Armed Robbery. These charges are independent, and the evidence should be considered separately for each charge.

In your consideration of the evidence regarding the offense of conspiracy, you should first determine whether or not the conspiracy existed, as alleged in the indictment. If you conclude that the conspiracy did exist, you should next deterrnine whether or not the defendant knowingly became a member of the conspiracy.

There may be liability even though the conspirators do not succeed in accomplishing their common object. In order for a conspiracy to be proven, it is not necessary that the prosecution show that the conspirators succeeded.

To prove the existence of a conspiracy, the State need not show the making of an express or formal agreement. Nor need the State prove that all the means set forth in the indictment were agreed upon, nor that all the means agreed upon were actually used, nor that each and every person charged as a member of a muiti-party conspiracy was such. The State must only prove the elements of conspiracy as defined in the previous instruction.

Mere Association Not Sufficient for Conspiracy

The fact that persons conduct themselves in a similar manner or associate with each other or assemble together or discuss common aims does not alone prove a conspiracy.

Lesser-Included Offense

The crime of Conspiracy to Commit Armed Robbery includes the lesser offense of Conspiracy to Commit Theft. You may consider the lesser offense of Conspiracy to Commit Theft if either:

1. You find the defendant not guilty of Conspiracy to Commit Armed Robbery; *or*

2. After full and careful consideration of the facts, you cannot agree on whether to find the defendant guilty or not guilty of Conspiracy to Commit Armed Robbery.

You cannot find the defendant guilty of Conspiracy to Commit Theft unless you find that the State has proved each element of Conspiracy to Commit Theft beyond a reasonable doubt.

Conspiracy to Commit Theft

The crime of conspiracy to commit theft requires proof of the following things:

1. That the defendant agreed with one or more persons that one of them or another person would engage in certain conduct; *and*

2. That the defendant intended to promote or assist the commission of such conduct; *and*

3. That the intended conduct would constitute the crime of Theft.

Armed Robbery

The crime of armed robbery requires proof of the following two things:

1. The defendant committed a robbery; *and*

2. The defendant or an accomplice was armed with a firearm.

Robbery

The crime of robbery requires proof of the following four things:

1. The defendant took another person's property; *and*

2. The taking was from the other person's person or immediate presence; *and*

3. The taking was against the other person's will; *and*

4. The defendant threatened or used force against any person with the intent to coerce surrender of the property or to prevent resistance to taking or keeping the property.

"Force" means any physical act directed against a person as a means of gaining control of property.

Lesser-Included Offense

The crime of Armed Robbery includes the lesser offense of Theft. You may consider the lesser offense of Theft if either:

1. You find the defendant not guilty of Armed Robbery; *or*

2. After full and careful consideration of the facts, you cannot agree on whether to find the defendant guilty or not guilty of Armed Robbery.

You cannot find the defendant guilty of Theft unless you find that the State has proved each element of Theft beyond a reasonable doubt.

Theft By Control With Intent To Deprive

The crime of theft requires proof of the following two things:

1. The defendant, without lawful authority, knowingly controlled another person's property; *and*

2. The defendant intended to deprive the other person of the property.

Dangerous Offense

A dangerous offense is one which involves the discharge, use, or threatening exhibition of a deadly weapon or dangerous instrument or the intentional infliction of serious physical injury upon another.

"Deadly Weapon" means anything designed for lethal use. The term includes a firearm.

"Firearm" means any loaded or unloaded handgun, pistol, revolver, rifle, shotgun or other weapon which will or is designed to or may readily be converted to expel a projectile by the action of expanding gases, except that it does not include a firearm in permanently inoperable condition.

Flight or Concealment

In determining whether the State has proved the defendant guilty beyond a reasonable doubt, you may consider any evidence of the defendant's running away, hiding, or concealing evidence, together with all the other evidence in the case. You may also consider the defendant's reasons for running away, hiding, or concealing evidence. Running away, hiding, or concealing evidence after a crime has been committed does not by itself prove guilt.

Final Instruction

I want to give you some final rules to guide you in your consideration of this case.

1. The first thing you should do is choose a presiding juror. The presiding juror will preside over your deliberations and will sign any verdict.

2. Do not take a vote until you have discussed all the evidence in the case.

3. You are to decide the case based upon the testimony and evidence that has been presented and your memories and notes of the testimony. You will not receive a transcript of the witnesses' testimony nor will you be able to hear additional testimony from the witnesses.

4. You are to decide this case without sympathy, bias or prejudice. You are to carefully and impartially consider all of the evidence in this case and follow the law as stated in these instructions and attempt to reach a verdict, regardless of the consequences. You took an oath promising to do so at the beginning of the case.

5. To return a verdict, all of you must agree on the verdict. All twelve of you must agree whether the verdict is guilty or not guilty.

6. Any questions you may have during deliberations should be submitted to the Court in writing by using the form provided to you by the Bailiff. Do not indicate on the question form the outcome of any vote that has been taken. If you feel you have reached an impasse, simply let the Court know without disclosing the numerical result of any vote.

You will be given five forms of verdict. I will now read those forms of verdict to you. You must understand that there is no significance to the order in which I read these verdicts.

Appendix 8

IMPASSE INSTRUCTIONS

Each juror has a duty to consult with one another, to deliberate with a view to reaching an agreement if it can be done without violence to individual judgment. No juror should surrender his or her honest conviction as to the weight or effect of the evidence solely because of the opinion of other jurors or for the purpose of reaching a verdict.

However, you may want to identify areas of agreement and disagreement and discuss the law and the evidence as they relate to the areas of disagreement.

If you still disagree, you may wish to tell the attorneys and me which issues, questions, law, or facts you would like us to assist you with. If you decide to follow this suggestion, please write down the issues, questions, law or facts on which we can possibly help. Please give your note to the bailiff. We will then discuss your note and try to help.

Appendix 9

Appendix 10

EXHIBITS PROVIDED TO JURY

Exhibit Number	Item
17	Photo of classified ads found in Cadillac
27	Smith & Wesson 9mm pistol
28	Bullet recovered from victim
30	Jewelry tags
36	Business card from Toyota 4/Runner
37	Jewelry tags
41	Copy of printout of room status
43	Copy of registration card
44	Copy of receipt for Chopard watch
45	Classified ad section of newspaper
46	Black gym bag
48	Recording of jail telephone call
50	**Photo of male subject in hallway outside vending room**
51	**Photo of female subject in vending room**
52	**Photo of front desk**
53	**Photo of circular drive**
54	**Diagram of crime scene**
56	Diagram of location of gunshot wound
58	**Photo of Chopard watch**
66	Defense video

Items in bold are reproduced in Appendix 11

Appendix 11

IMAGES OF KEY EXHIBITS
FROM TRIAL

Exhibit Number	Item
50	Surveillance Camera Photo: Male subject in Hallway Outside Vending Room
51	Surveillance Camera Photo: Female subject in Vending Room
52	Surveillance Camera Photo: Front Desk
53	Surveillance Camera Photo: Circular Drive
54	Diagram of Crime Scene
58	Photo of Chopard Watch

Exhibit 50

CAM 10 · 02- 9- 8 THU 21:55:45 24H

Exhibit 51

CAM 10 · 02- 9- 8 THU 22:03:45 24H

Exhibit 52

CAM 2 02- 8- 8 THU 21:34:17 L24H

Exhibit 53

CAM 6 02- 8- 8 THU 21:34:38 L24H

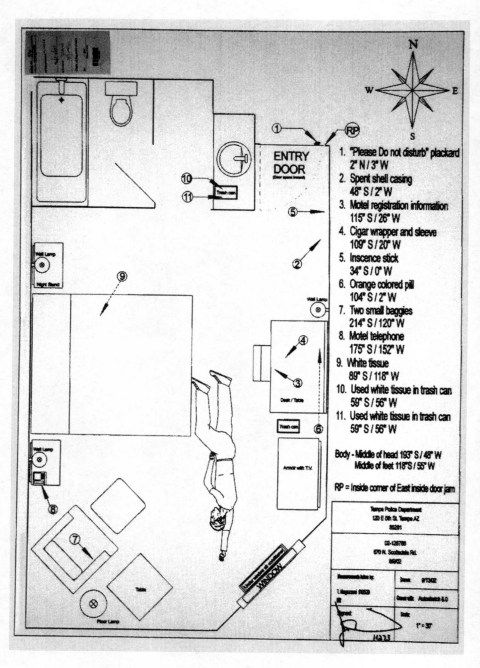

1. "Please Do not disturb" plackard
   2" N / 3" W
2. Spent shell casing
   48" S / 2" W
3. Motel registration information
   115" S / 26" W
4. Cigar wrapper and sleeve
   109" S / 20" W
5. Inscence stick
   34" S / 0" W
6. Orange colored pill
   104" S / 2" W
7. Two small baggies
   214" S / 120" W
8. Motel telephone
   175" S / 152" W
9. White tissue
   89" S / 118" W
10. Used white tissue in trash can
    59" S / 56" W
11. Used white tissue in trash can
    59" S / 56" W

Body - Middle of head 193" S / 48" W
       Middle of feet 118"S / 55" W

RP = Inside corner of East inside door jam

Exhibit 54

Exhibit 58

Appendix 12

PHOTO OF DEFENDANT AT TIME OF ARREST

Robert Lemke

50987067R00081

Made in the USA
Charleston, SC
08 January 2016